CHASING THE WIND

Memories of a TV Meteorologist

Author: George Winterling

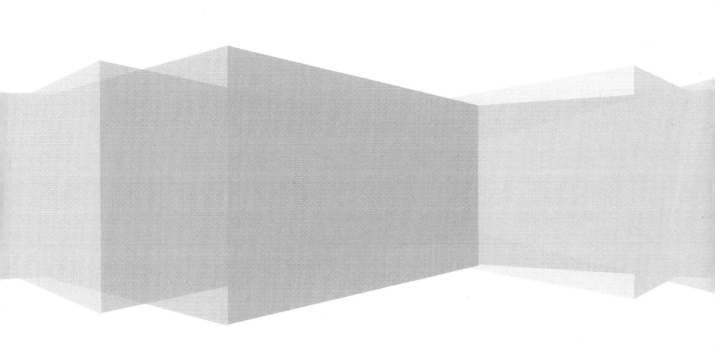

To my wife and soul mate, Virginia

INTRODUCTION

In our early years, we read about history. In our later years, we become history.

Then comes the sad realization that we never asked our grandparents or even our parents how they met each other, what their childhoods were like, or what was new, happy, sad, frightening, or exciting in their adult lives. No, we never gave it much thought; until they were gone.

So to my grandchildren and beyond, when you become my age and wonder what your ancestors were like; no worries — here I am.

Read how my life's journey took me from exploring virgin woods, rural and small-town life in the garden state of New Jersey to five decades as a pioneer broadcast meteorologist at Florida's second oldest television station WJXT-TV4 in Jacksonville, Florida.

And know, that as I enter the twilight of my life, I have been thinking of you. I have tried to recall my adventures from childhood and family life to manhood and career. This memoir is an attempt to record for you some of the steps I took while walking this long journey in life before the passage of time caused these memories to fade.

You're welcome!

TABLE OF CONTENTS

CHAPTER 01 - Childhood Days

On September 1, 1931, I was born in Pine Beach, NJ in a house on US 9, the main highway between New York City and Atlantic City. My earliest thoughts about life occurred one day when I was less than two years old. As I stood on the lawn looking at the pine trees, the sky, and the cars passing by, I wondered where I came from. It was not until I became a young adult that the first piece to the puzzle fell into place.

In 1951, my grandfather, George Winterling, wrote me a detailed letter describing his life and our family history going back to the middle of the 19th century. The European family roots are in Ashe, the Czech Republic near the Black Forest.

As a young man, he took a job in nearby Oelsnitz, Germany, where he met and married Laura Jakel. Together, they had three children; my father, Otto Gustav, a second son, Beno, and a daughter, Rosa.

The Winterling home in Belgium before moving to the United States

Around 1910, the family moved to Belgium, from which he was later transferred to a German Tapestry company in Toronto, Canada. When his contract expired in 1914, being aware of the threat of war in Europe, he decided to settle in the United States. The family came through the Buffalo, New York Port of Entry and headed to Florida where they moved into a cabin in Wauchula to try their hand at growing sugar beets.

Laura Winterling likely Pine Beach property near George's Sonoco gas Station

Being unsuccessful at farming, my grandfather headed north to Philadelphia where he worked as a loom repairman for a carpet factory. In 1925 he bought property in Pine Beach, New Jersey at US 9 and Motor Road. He operated a Sunoco Service Station to which he added a restaurant and bar. He and my father built a large two-story boarding house with tourist cabins, a very successful business on the main highway between New York City and Atlantic City.

PINE BEACH SERVICE STATION
George Winterling - Prop.
A.C BLVD and PINE BEACH ENTRANCE
PINE BEACH

Otto Gustav Winterling   around 1930

As a young man, my father, Otto Gustav Winterling, taught manual training (shop) at nearby Barnegat High School. He and a fellow teacher, Harry Allen, had a speedboat powered by a Ford V-8 engine that he took me and my brother, Richard, for rides on the Toms River.

Harry and my father would spend their summers traveling and fishing. My father loved fly-fishing. He used a long flexible pole that had a line that allowed him to swirl an insect-looking bait above the water. When the lure struck the water, the trout would charge at it.

I remember one summer when he brought back movies of his trip to California, showing pictures of Old Faithful at Yellowstone National Park and of himself and Harry being dwarfed by a giant Redwood tree. I remember one picture of the huge Sequoia that had a tunnel carved through its base that was large enough to drive a car through.

My father went on to attend Rutgers University before meeting my mother Ruth Cranmer. She grew up on a family farm in southern Jersey. The Cranmers had come from England in the early 19th century, eventually settling in Mayetta. Ruth was one of Frank and Mary Cranmer's four children. She attended Normal School to become an elementary teacher, similar to her brother, Clinton, and sister, Hazel. Upon marrying my father, she moved into my grandfather Winterling's boarding house where my brother, Richard, and I were born.

My earliest notable experience was being told that as a bare-foot baby in diapers I walked from our home a distance of twenty-five yards to my grandparent's restaurant. They were shocked to see me since there was snow covering the ground. My first memory as a baby was being placed in my crib one day. I didn't want to go to sleep. I started crying and even cried harder as I saw my mother ignore me by walking out of the room.

GEORGE & RICHARD WINTERLING

One side of the bedroom had a large window facing heavily traveled US 9. After dark, I was puzzled by the sight of strange "creatures" moving across windows. I later learned that these were shadows of trees and shrubs on the curtains produced by the headlights of cars passing by on the highway.

At the age of two, I was joined by baby brother Richard. I couldn't say "Richard". All that I could say was "Chee-Chee". Being 21 months older than him, I didn't remember much of his early childhood. I was always looking for things to do. I had the curiosity of a cat and probably also more than one life.

One day I found my father's safety razor in the bathroom. While playing with it and I soon found that my thumb was colored red with blood. Another day as my father was cutting grass with a scythe (a large long bladed grass-cutting tool), I got too close as my father was mowing. The blade hit my cheek near the eye. Consequently, I had my first trip to the doctor for stitches, thankful that it didn't hit my eye.

4

1934 - I had a ball when my Dad taught me to swim in the Toms River.

I was about three years old when I tried to walk around my grandfather's gas station with my eyes closed. I only made it halfway around when I suddenly tripped on the rim of the oil pit which cars drove over to have their oil changed. I tumbled into the pit, landing head first into a tub of crankcase oil. I scrambled up the concrete steps, crying as I ran to my grandfather. My mother shortly was trying to remove my blackened complexion by giving me a thorough scrubbing in the bathtub. Not long after that, I explored our medicine cabinet and discovered the most delicious chocolate candy.

I couldn't hide from my mother the fact I had eaten all of it. It was the laxative, Ex-Lax. That was one time I was thoroughly clean, inside and out!

One day, I got a shovel and proceeded to dig a hole as deep as I could because I wanted to see China! That was the hot summer day that my family laughingly remembers. At dinner time they were all surprised when I got up from the dinner table and ran in circles around the kitchen. My grandfather later learned from his bartender that several times that afternoon I had been spotted going behind the bar a couple of times to the beer tap, pouring myself a swig of the brew. Behind the house, between the bar and the cabins, was an old Model A or Model T truck. It had a belt attached to the rear wheel that was probably attached to a saw for cutting lumber. We didn't pay much attention to the rear of the truck, but it was just perfect for Richard and me to climb up into the front seat to take turns sitting behind the steering wheel, pretending that we were driving.

We loved to visit our other grandparents' farm in Mayetta. One of the most unforgettable sights was watching my mother's mother, Mamie Cranmer, whom we called Me-mom select a chicken for Sunday dinner. She would select a plump chicken, lay its head on an old tree stump, and chop its head off. I know she got a kick out of watching us laugh our heads off as the headless chicken running around the yard. One day Richard discovered that roosters were not friendly. He got pecked a few times as the rooster charged him.

5

Between the driveway and the kitchen was a large walnut tree. I have many memories of eating cool watermelon on hot summer days.

The only thing that topped it was when my uncle, Clinton Cranmer, drove up with a basket of clams from Barnegat Bay.

We especially loved eating the raw clams as he shucked them under the giant Walnut tree outside my grandmother's kitchen door. We also watched Me-mom chop them in a wooden bowl, beat some eggs, and then fry some mouth-watering clam fritters.

Wherever I've gone since I've never found any clams as tasty as that!

1920 GEORGE AND LAURA WINTERLING

CHAPTER 02 - Expanding My World

1935 Winterling home - 2 sons at fence

Our house was a mile from the Toms River with mostly woods between. There were a couple of gravel pits and a trash dump on the west side of Motor Road. The main activity was along the Atlantic City highway adjacent to our house. I thought it was interesting to hear and watch the chains under the heavier trucks moving as they drove the rear wheels.

One day I saw a truck stopping by each telephone pole. A man was hammering glass reflectors into the pole to reflect the car headlights at night. Most of the time, I loved to roam through the woods on the east side of Motor Road all the way down to the railroad tracks. I'd discover paths and trails and paused occasionally to snack on some blueberries and huckleberries in the native vegetation. Every once in a while I'd discover a special treat…a delicious teaberry!

I enjoyed strolling along the shore of the river that had a bank lined with a short wall consisting of concrete-filled bags. I watched the water as miniature waves that rolled and disappeared into the gravel beach, and especially the larger ones that arrived following the passage of a speedboat offshore.

I liked watching people catch crabs from the dock. One day I asked my grandmother for a piece of meat and string. Taking a bucket and net from the basement, I joined the others at the pier. What fond memories I have of bringing in a bucket-full of crabs and watching my grandmother dump the crabs into the scalding water on the kitchen stove. Eating the sweet crab meat at the end of a day at the river was the high point of my summers in Pine Beach.

My grandfather had tourist cabins for the travelers that came from points north to the Jersey shore. Above one building was a water tank and inside was a piece of machinery with a large wheel and a belt that ran to a pulley. We didn't know it ran the pump that filled the tank. As children, we would try turning the wheel to try to make it spin. Luckily the pump never started while we were playing with it. My grandfather always enjoyed improving the property he had developed at the corner of Motor Road and the Atlantic City US 9 highway. One of his projects was building a 350 ft. picket fence around his house. I was fascinated watching him of mix the concrete and pour it into a mold for the fence posts. Forty years later and 24 years after his passing in 1952, I returned to view the abandoned house. The fence was no longer there, but I retrieved one of the concrete posts for a memorial of his life at my home in Jacksonville, FL.

One day in 1937 while returning from the river down the path in the woods, I heard a hum in the sky and saw something that looked like a large gray cloud through the tree branches. I curiously ran to a small clearing by the railroad tracks and recognized that it was a dirigible that appeared to be only a thousand feet above the Toms River. The enormity of it and the low monotone hum of the motors sounded very ominous to me.

A couple of hours later while eating dinner in the kitchen of our home, we heard a loud rumble. My grandfather ran outside thinking his water tank had collapsed. Seeing black smoke in the direction of Lakehurst, we all got in the car and drove to the Naval Station. I remember looking through the fence at the edge of the airport and seeing the haunting frame of the airship with the wreckage beneath it still smoldering.
I had remembered during those days in the 1930's of seeing calendars with a picture of a tilted dirigible on a date when the Graf Zeppelin crashed. When I was growing up, we didn't receive toys or presents apart from birthdays and Christmas. But one day when I met my grandfather returning Philadelphia, he presented me with a Gyroscope. This strange contraption had a solid metal wheel inside a stiff wire container. After winding a string around its axis, a swift pull would accelerate the wheel to cause an inexplicable force. The gyroscope would resist any effort to turn it from its plane of rotation. This taught me how the property of angular momentum is useful in navigation for airplanes, ships, and spacecraft.

In 1937, we moved to Plainfield, NJ where I started the first grade in school. My mother was a school teacher, and my father also taught school, but it was at Barnegat High on the Jersey shore between Pine Beach and Mayetta. He was an excellent craftsman who taught Manual Training there. He had an easy-going temperament which was not a good fit for dealing with some of his rowdy high school students. A couple of years later he joined us in Cranford after spending a few months with a nervous breakdown in a sanitarium not far from Scotch Plains.

Upon completing the first grade, I spent the summer exploring the neighborhood. One day I decided to brighten it up. I spied our landlord's old Essex automobile which had wooden spokes on its wheels. I decided that they would look better colored red, so I decided to paint them. I often wondered why we then had to move!

While I was in the second grade at Scotch Plains, NJ, I remember a few of our projects in school. I thought it was neat to separate cardboard layers and glue them to the side of the jar with the corrugated part on the outside. We then painted them and shellacked them to give them a glazed appearance. They were nice for display at school and to have at home to contain some of my stuff. Another project was to place a moistened slice of bread into a jar, seal it and place it in a dark closet. Several days later, the bread turned a greenish-gray, covered with a growth of mold.

I remember one day in class a classmate, Charlie, kept getting up to run his pencil in the pencil sharpener. After three or four trips, the teacher finally asked Charlie why he kept sharpening his pencil. Charlie said it was because the fresh wood on the lower part of the pencil kept getting dirty.

I would sometimes go home for lunch around noon. One day while crossing one of the main intersections in town, I noticed the cars approaching, waiting, and then passing through. For some reason, I decided to go back home, change into a blue shirt. Then armed with a toy badge from a Cracker Jack, I proceeded back to the middle of the intersection where it I stood directing the traffic waving my arms and blowing a whistle.

That summer I caught "poison ivy", a very uncomfortable skin rash that itched incessantly. My mother got Fels-Naptha soap and scrubbed my skin to rid me of the allergic reaction. I thought it strange that my brother, Richard, never got it. Apparently, he was immune to it.

A kid has no more fun than feeling the rain on the face and stomping in mud puddles. One rainy September day, I spotted a low spot on the road with a rain-swollen ditch. Always loving to swim, I climbed over the railing of the bridge to get into the water. But when I lowered myself over the railing by the sidewalk, I discovered the current was flowing into a culvert under the road. I gripped the railing but was unable to pull myself back to the sidewalk. Fortunately, a driver spotted my dilemma, stopped, and lifted me up to safety. I then recalled that I had heard flood warnings on the radio and thought they were just for the mountains in northern New Jersey. The next day, I learned that New England was struck by a disastrous storm, the infamous hurricane of 1938.

Airplanes and the clouds always fascinated me. Occasionally, I would look up at the blue sky and see a sky-writing plane spell out Coca-Cola. I wouldn't miss the comic strips with airplanes and airships, like Smilin' Jack and Tailspin Tommy. One day my father drove us to Newark airport to see them on the ground. Wow! What a sight to see a bright silver DC-3 Eastern Air Lines plane parked by the terminal.

When the next Christmas came, my father gave me a wood-burning kit. It had an electrically heated pen and a few slabs of softwood containing drawings of a bird or an animal. The object of the kit was to burn each image into the boards. My first lesson

1939 Georgie and Richie at Cranford, NJ gas station

was a painful one, not to hold the lower end of the pen below its cork ring. The first time I held it, the heated end burned my fingers. A few weeks prior to that Christmas, I remembered watching my grandmother (Grosmutter) knitting from large spools of maroon wool.

On the morning that Santa arrived, I unwrapped a present that contained a pair of nice, warm wool stockings. I was very happy because when walking outside my feet had been getting numb from the cold, damp winter weather.

In 1939, we moved to 54 Hillcrest Avenue in Cranford, NJ. Next to the house was a short concrete-paved slope that I wanted to use for sledding; however, we never had enough snow to cover the entire pavement. One morning following an overnight snow, I thought there was enough packed snow on it for a good slide, but just as I slid ten or twelve feet the runners would hit the bare concrete and screech to a halt.

That was the year that I tried to earn some money selling Christmas cards. I had no printed cards, so I created some home-made ones. On the front, I drew a star over some yellow scratches to look like hay, and inside I wrote a verse that simply said, "And it came to pass". I couldn't understand why some people laughed when they read it.

A few days later when my brother Richard was outside, I locked the kitchen door. When my brother Richard failed to get in, he picked up an ax and tried to chop the door open. Shortly afterward, we moved to North Avenue West where I thought I would do something nice for my brother. Having seen my mother write checks when making a purchase, I took a blank one and wrote it for 25 dollars. I went to the store in town to buy my brother a red bicycle for his birthday. The store owner called mother and canceled the sale!

It was in Cranford that I started taking piano lessons. After learning to play the "Joyous Peasant", I was saddened to learn that my parents couldn't afford lessons anymore.
I always loved music. Years later I taught myself enough to play some hymns in church, but only simple songs with very few sharp or flat keys. My school had a small orchestra and I was encouraged to learn the violin. I could never learn how to keep it from screeching!

The New York World's Fair in 1939 was a spectacular event. Daddy took Richard and me there. It was a beautiful sight walking through the entrance toward the brilliant blue reflecting pool, lined with the colorful flags of many nations. Beyond that was the spear-like Trylon and the large globe called the Perisphere. This was a predecessor of Disney's Epcot globe in Orlando. Inside was a model of a utopian city. We viewed it from a moving sidewalk that made it feel like we were looking down from an airplane or airship.

1940 George Winterling 4th grade picture

In 1940 I was introduced to politics. Wendell Wilkie was the Republican candidate opposing Franklin Roosevelt, who was running for an unprecedented third term. For some reason, the name Wilkie captured my fancy and I considered myself a Wilkie fan. I was disappointed when I learned that FDR had won.

Walking to and from school, I always walked by the U.S. Post Office. They had a large picture of Uncle Sam facing the sidewalk saying "I Want You". What was so unique was the way that the finger pointed out. Whichever way I walked by the sign, it looked like the finger was always pointing at me.

Like many kids, we were always exploring the town. Not far from the Cleveland Elementary School I attended, there was an ancient red brick school building that had closed. It was always very spooky whenever I peeked through the dingy windows into the dark building. Mother always told us to stay away from trash cans and the garbage dump. But the urge to discover hidden treasure led us to search anyway. When we would find empty tin cans, we would select two the right size to fit around our shoes. We laid them on their sides and stomp them so the edges would clamp to the side of our soles, much as roller skates would. We could then walk on the sidewalk, making a clomping sound like the tin man in the Wizard of Oz.

I never had a lot of playmates. I usually picked one that I felt close to so we could share our thoughts and feelings with each other. There was one that I felt was my friend. I can't remember if his first name or last name was Howard, but after I spent a few days walking around town with him, my mother told me she thought I shouldn't be seen with him. When I asked why she replied: "Because he's a negro". I had always accepted him as a nice kid and couldn't understand what was wrong with having a negro for a playmate.

One day around noon, I was walking a block away from school and I saw a few classmates were talking. After joining them, one of the boys looked at me and said, "It's 2 o'clock at the waterworks". I was surprised to hear that it was that late, so I said I have to go home. When I got home, I discovered that it was only one o'clock. I couldn't understand why they said two o'clock until I went to the bathroom and discovered there were two buttons on my fly that were not buttoned!

My mother's sister, Hazel Woodfield, was a school teacher in Asbury Park. Her present to me on my birthday was "The Wonder Book of Knowledge", a book that answered almost any question an inquisitive kid would ask. My brother Richard and I always enjoyed staying with her each summer. The boardwalk in Asbury Park was the "Disneyland" of that era. We especially remembered driving the motor boats, pressing the accelerator and steering the motor boats inside a fenced area. Next to the lake was the amusement park with the huge Merry-Go-Round and a ride that went through a darkened tunnel. It was called The Fun House, but it was very spooky.

In the darkness, we caught flickering sights of scary figures followed by the sensation of invisible strings brushing across our faces. When we rode the giant Ferris wheel nearby, we were carried well above the roof of the building. From the lofty ride could view nearby Ocean Grove and the blue waters of the Atlantic Ocean. Many times at family gatherings, Aunt Hazel would relate my 4-year old brother's experience when the Ferris Wheel stopped with a jerk at the top. He suddenly said, "Oh sh...t"! It was evident that he learned the expression from our grandfather, Frank Cranmer, at the farmhouse in Mayetta. I remember my grandmother chastising her husband one day when he stated that he was going out in the cornfield behind the "sh…t house".

Our mother's brother Clinton Cranmer was a school teacher in Paterson, NJ. When he drove in his freshly Simonized Chrysler to Mayetta, he would stop in Cranford to pick up Richard and me to visit the farm. As we drove past Perth Amboy, we saw a beautiful orange-roofed building that had a sign stating that it had 28 ice cream flavors. That was the first Howard Johnson's we had ever seen or stopped at.

A few days before Christmas when I was nine years old, I dropped a marble on the bedroom floor. Reaching down to pick it up, I spotted a set of skis under the bed. Obviously, I wasn't surprised when I saw them by the tree on Christmas morning. I was more excited by my new electric Lionel Train. I often experimented with ways to run it, even unscrewing the locomotive's top and just racing the electric motor and wheels off a stretch of raised tracks that sent it flying across the room.

CHAPTER 03 - Leaving New Jersey

As a fourth grader in 1941, I was surprised to learn that we were moving to Florida. When I heard this, I imagined it was like a jungle with large trees and vines with monkeys. I excitedly told many of my classmates at Cranford's Cleveland School that I would write about my new world. I wrote their addresses on a thick red tablet. When we arrived in Green Cove Springs, Florida, I asked my mother where the tablet was. I was shocked when she told me she didn't know. Not finding it made me feel like I was cut off from the many friends I had in New Jersey.

1941 Georgie moves to Florida

We lived in a one-room frame building on a field about a mile west of the springs in Green Cove Springs. My father worked as a carpenter at Benjamin Lee Field, a U.S. Navy base about a mile south of the town.

I thought I would die of thirst the first few months. We got our water from a water faucet on a pipe about 50 feet from our cabin. The water tasted horrible...like rotten eggs! I learned that it was sulfur water. To make it more palatable, we chilled it in a glass bottle in the refrigerator to reduce the yucky taste.

The heat and humidity, not to mention the intensity of the sunshine, prompted me and my brother, Richard, to spend most days at the swimming pool in town by the spring. Even though the water reeked of sulfur, it was cool and refreshing. The white building next to the pool had black lines with numbers on the wall. There was an edge of a shadow of an adjacent wall slowly moved to mark the hour of the day. This was a unique form of "sundial" that told us the time during the many hours we spent at the pool.

Around mid-summer, we moved to St. Augustine, which was not as hot because it was closer to the ocean. We lived only a few blocks from the historical sites, such as the Castillo De San Marcos and the Old Schoolhouse. Every few days I headed to the hobby shop to purchase a new model airplane kit because as soon as I finished building one, I needed another one to build. Upon returning home on one showery afternoon, I was told a small tornado knocked a chimney off a nearby house. I couldn't understand how a wind could do that when I didn't observe any other debris in the neighborhood. Years later as a meteorologist, I learned that many of our Florida tornadoes are often so small and isolated, they sometimes just rip through a few tree branches and touch down only briefly.

CHAPTER 04 - Settling in Jacksonville

The year was 1941. Having learned carpentry from his father in Pine Beach, my father got a Civil Service job in the Maintenance Building at Benjamin Lee Auxiliary Field in Green Cove Springs. He and Edgar Clancy, an electrician, became good friends. When World War II started, much more gasoline was needed for the war and gasoline had to be rationed in the U.S. He had a bigger allotment than others because he had a sticker on his windshield with a large "A" displayed.

My family bought a new house off Timuquana Road, a little over a mile from the new Jacksonville Naval Air Station. With only a dozen new homes finished, the builder dug a large eighteen-inch deep hole, built a fire in it, and placed the carcass of a large pig on a metal grate above the fire. It was there that I was introduced to the mouth-watering southern tradition of eating barbeque.

1943 Richard and George in front of our Timuquana home

My growing interest in aviation was further increased as I frequently saw bright yellow double-winged Stearman airplanes overhead. They would circle over our neighborhood when they practiced landing and taking off at the nearby airbase.

During the war years, the skies over our neighborhood gradually changed. Soon there were no more Stearman trainers. Instead, we heard the buzz and saw the short, stubby F4F Grumman Wildcats, a plane with narrow wheels the protruded from the fuselage. In school, we were encouraged to be patriotic. War stamps were sold to paste in a booklet that contained enough spaces to total $18.75, enough to exchange for a $25 War Bond. We also collected newspapers so that after several months we had a stack of papers as high as I could barely reach, about six feet. A paper company, R.V. Sutphin, paid us over fifteen dollars for them, enough to purchase a lot of war stamps. Soon I had enough stamps to cash them in for a $25 war bond.

As the war effort increased and aviation advanced, we saw the small Wildcats replaced by larger torpedo bombers. The Grumman TBF or TBM Avengers flew in formations as they returned from target practice over the Atlantic. They would peel off to the left from the group to circle the field for landing. Unfortunately, one day the pilot of the second plane in the formation mistakenly thought the first one had already peeled off. Tragically, he peeled and rammed into the first plane. Both pilots were killed when their doomed planes nose-dived into the swamp less than one-half mile from my house. My brother, Richard, heard and saw the disaster as he was with the School Boy patrol guarding the crosswalk at nearby Venetia Elementary School.

When we headed down Timuquana Road towards the river and Timuquana Country Club to the fence of the Navy base, we sometimes spotted a plane trailing a long rope attached to a white silk target that was used to train fighter pilots. When they approached the airfield, they would release the tow rope so the target could drop between the runway and the fence. We often gathered there to see how close to the fence the target would land. One day the wind blew the target onto our side of the fence. We thought we had obtained a souvenir, but as we carried it through the woods to Roosevelt Blvd, a car stopped and a Navy officer got out and took it from us.

Living on Blount Avenue in Timuquana Manor provided me with a world of adventure. One-half mile down Timuquana Road was McGirts Creek (now called Ortega River).

One block past the bridge over the creek was Williams' store where we reached into a soft drink box of crushed ice and ice cold water to fish out a 12-ounce bottle of Pepsi Cola or RC Cola. On hot summer days, we were refreshed by a cold drink and a Ward's Tip-Top Chocolate Devil's Food Cake. It had a marshmallow center that made it really yummy. The taste was very much like today's Little Debbie Swiss Rolls.

We often bought a loaf of bread, using pieces from the soft white center for bait to fish for bream and shiners. We carried the bream home to eat, but if we were lucky enough to catch a shiner, would use it as live bait to catch a bass. I tried to catch one unsuccessfully for several years. Finally, after five years I dropped a hand-line with a shiner from the high point of the bridge. The float bobbed for about a half hour. Suddenly, I saw my float rapidly move away. I slowly counted to ten and then yanked the line to hook the fish. Standing on the bridge about 20 feet above the water, I slowly pulled on the line, hand over hand. As I hoisted it from the water up to the bridge railing, all I could see was the large mouth of the fish with my line disappearing deep in its throat. I couldn't wait to get home to show everyone the prize I had caught.

We usually walked bare-footed from the bridge to our home on Blount Avenue. The hot summer sun often melted the asphalt (tar) pavement so that it would stick to our feet. When an occasional car came by, we had to step aside, often into a patch of sandspurs. Often during the hot summer, the sandspurs were so thick that we had to endure the pain of walking on the gummy asphalt. We wore tennis shoes to explore the woods off Timuquana Road. Our neighborhood was separated from Ortega Forest by a small lake called Loon Lake. It was surrounded by drainage ditches and a corner with a few small hills covered with pine straw. We could slide down these slopes on the slick pine needles as easily as if it was snow. To circle the lake, we'd have to jump over several drainage ditches, often soaking our shoes when we landed in the soggy muck. We never saw a snake or alligator in the years we explored those wilds, although I sure a few of them had spotted us.

The Atlantic Coast Line railroad was a couple of blocks to the east. When we heard a train coming, we'd put a penny on the tracks to see what the locomotive would do to it. After the train passed, we'd find a hot, flattened piece of copper that once was the coin. In later years, I wished I had saved one of the silver-colored zinc pennies that were only minted in 1943. In those days all of us kids had comic books, like Superman, Batman, and Captain Marvel. Whenever we went to their homes, there was usually a stack of

18

them in a corner or on a table. On rainy days, we'd get tired of the comic books, so we then played card games like Old Maid, Slapjack or Rummy. A few of us had pets. I had a Collie-Spaniel mix that I named Champ, after Gene Autry's horse Champion. At times he would come in from the woods with a blood-filled tick on his back that I had to pull off. One day, Champ went under a neighbor's house and wouldn't come out. He snarled at us when we called him. That was the last that I saw him because he had gotten rabies and had to be put to sleep.

During the cold winter, we would collect pieces of coal beside the railroad track that had fallen from the coal car behind the locomotive. I didn't think the fireman who shoveled the coal into the flames of the furnace on the locomotive could retrieve them. We put good use of the coal in our fireplace to heat our home. The rails were our hiking path north to the Ortega River and south to Orange Park. We would see how far we could walk on the rails without falling off.

A mile and a half south of Timuquana Road was the entrance to Jacksonville Naval Air Station. Since my father worked at Lee Field (in Green Cove Springs), and several of my friends were apparently children of Navy personnel, we were allowed to swim at the pools at NAS. We swam in two of the main side pools most of the time and a couple of times in the officers' pool. Adjacent to the main side pool was the theatre where we watched movies, such as the Bing Crosby-Bob Hope films. After the movie go into BX (Base Exchange) and buy a large milkshake for only ten cents. This really topped off a day at the pool, movies and ice cream fountain.

At times we would head down Timuquana Road to the bulkhead on the bank of the St Johns River to watch the PBY Catalina seaplanes practice taking off and landing in the river. The designation PB stood for "patrol boat", and the Y stood for the aircraft company (Consolidated) that built it. They said there were more PBYs built than any other during World War II. Some were built with retractable wheels so they could be used anywhere in the world – on land or on water. Once we saw a gigantic seaplane, the Martin Mariner. It was unique not only for its size but also because it had gull-shaped wings.

When I visited the home of my sixth-grade classmate, Jimmy Butts, I saw him make model airplanes from sticks of balsa wood. Being an avid aviation enthusiast, I picked up the hobby. Every Saturday, after catching the city bus (fare 5 cents) to town to watch a western movie (9 cents), buy a Krystal hamburger (7 cents) and Orange Crush drink

(5 cents), I would purchase a model airplane kit. It was usually a World War II plane. After a couple years, I had mounted the "squadrons" of model planes all over my bedroom on strings that stretched from wall to wall. I built one model of Kitty Hawk fame, flown by the Wright brothers. I constructed it from a photo of the historic flight, and the model actually flew when pulled by a light string.

Jimmy Butts' family lived in a house next to the Naval Baptist Church in Yukon, across Roosevelt Blvd. from the Naval Air Station. The church later was renamed Yukon Baptist Church. We both attended Sunday School there. We had a teacher, Bob Peterson, who encouraged us to memorize a scripture each week. At the end of each session, he'd hand each of us a business-size card with a hand-printed scripture verse on it. We carried it with us all week, and to this day I can still quote more than a dozen verses I learned as a teenager.

CHAPTER 05 - Family Life

Children in my generation generally lived in a different world than grownups. We pretty much played, either alone or with neighborhood playmates. Our interaction with parents was usually at mealtime, when we were sick, or when we had questions about our homework. This being World War II, we were urged to conserve food and materials for the war effort. Our car had an "A" sticker on the windshield to represent our allotment for gasoline. The top half of the headlights were painted black to keep the light from illuminating the sky for potential enemy warplanes. Our family had food ration booklets containing stamps for our allotment of things like meat, sugar, and butter. One day, Mother took some fresh vegetables to the Canning Kitchen. When she brought home the box of shiny tin cans, they had not been labeled. For the next few months, she didn't know what she was serving until she opened the can! She also planted English Peas and Cherry Tomatoes in a Victory Garden across our backyard. The peas and tomatoes were a tasty snack for us when taking a break from our outside activities. The games we played were Dodge Ball, Red Light, and Hide and Seek. We also exercised on a pipe connected to two trees for doing chin-ups.

During the war, our clocks were advanced one hour to conserve energy. It was called Eastern War Time. I remember playing softball outside in daylight as late as 9 PM but turning out the lights to go to bed an hour later at 10. We used no electricity to cool our homes because there was no air conditioning available in those days. We usually kept our windows open during warm days and nights. We depended on screens to keep the swarms of small flying insects out of the house, but we sometimes saw one at night flying inside an illuminated lampshade. One not so pleasant discovery occurred at dinnertime when we had just sat down at the table for supper. Suddenly, we heard a clink over our heads as one of the chains broke holding a glass shade on our ceiling light fixture. As the shade tilted downward, we received a shower of dead bugs!

Among our household chores was washing the dishes, making the beds, dusting the furniture and vacuuming the floors. We sometimes gathered outdoors with neighborhood kids to play softball or touch football, depending on the time of the year. On days when it was too cold, or raining, we stayed inside and played cards or read comic books. Not having TV, we only had a radio, but it did have interesting programs. We felt like cowboys when listening to Tom Mix and the Lone Ranger, or airplane pilots as we heard Hop Harrigan saying, "This is CX4 to control tower, calling for permission to land". We often spent the last hour of the day in the bedroom looking at the lighted numbers of our Silvertone radio dial as we listened to G-men going after the bad guys on Gang Busters, or the mystery behind the squeaking door on the Inner Sanctum.

I belonged to an "off and on" Boy Scout troop that had trouble keeping enough boys for meetings. Eventually, I earned enough merit badges by studying the manuals, doing the projects, and meeting with counselors to become a Life scout. I loved camping. Being outdoors, I could relate to the pioneers who discovered our country as I pitched the pup tent and built the campfire. I was fascinated with the battery-less crystal radio, which would simply operate from a copper wire antenna and a "cat's whisker" wire touching a piece of galena embedded in lead. We listened through headphones connected to a coil of wire around a paperless toilet paper core. When camping in the woods, I'd attach a string of copper wire antenna wire to a nearby tree for an antenna that enabled me to listen to the radio in my tent. Jacksonville had only four radio stations. WJAX the municipal station, WMBR, and WJHP the Jacksonville Journal station were the oldest ones. Then one day a new one joined the selections, WPDQ. We usually camped under the live oaks along McGirt's Creek (Ortega River) near a high point called the Bluff.

In order to receive more distant radio stations at my house, I decided to string a copper wire to a point as high as I could climb in the young pine tree outside my window. As I was about 12 feet above the ground in the tree holding the wire, I suddenly felt an electrical shock in my hand at the same instant there was a lightning flash in the distance. The lesson I learned was that ordinary electrical nature of the air can change even away from a distant lightning strike. Another thing I learned was I could detect a dial tone in my headphones when the antenna brushed against the telephone line. A few months later I decided to extend my antenna to a higher level. I cut down several pine saplings from the nearby woods and constructed a 30-foot tower.

In addition to radio, my interest in photography led me to obtain a Kodak Film Developing Kit. Since I needed a dark room, I used a storage loft in the rear of my garage. I used three trays to pass the film from the Developer to the Hypo solution, which stopped the developing and finally to the Fixer tray. I couldn't do much else without an enlarger. Years later while serving in the Air Force, I had access to photo developing facilities in the Hobby Shop at Elmendorf AFB in Alaska.

One of my Boy Scout requirements was to hike a few miles and camp out alone overnight. On that night it began to rain. After I pitched my tent and settled in for the night on my sleeping bag, water began to seep in under the side of the tent. Throughout the night, I began to see tiny green spots of light on the ground surrounding my covers. I feared that it was snakes that had crawled inside to escape the rain; however, I learned later that it was merely phosphorus glowing in the soggy oak twigs. Several years later I saw the same green phosphorus spots of light in the ocean waters that were churned up by the transport ship that was carrying me from San Francisco to my Air Force assignment in Alaska.

CHAPTER 06 - Before Television

This was the golden age of both radio and the movies. I used our old push mower and cut lawns to earn money for my hobby of building model airplanes. I charged 25 cents for a front yard and 50 cents for front and back. Several yards had tall thin weed heads that the reel-type lawn mower would not cut. I had to swing a weed-cutter that had a ratchet blade on the end of a 3-foot wooden pole. In the winter, I cut firewood and sold it to some of our neighbors. I also delivered magazines that were dropped off at our house. I delivered Collier's, a weekly magazine and Saturday Evening Post which was bi-weekly.

During the summer, my brother Richard and I would meet with playmates Henry Reckstein, Paul Crisp, Nancy Horning, and a few others to play softball on a vacant corner lot. Sometimes we played until it was too dark to see the ball. We met there for only a year or two because a new house was soon built on the lot. After that, we played war games on an undeveloped lot a block away. Being inspired by war movies and spies, we dug a trench by the campsite and covered it with boards and dirt to make it like an underground tunnel. One day, I cleaned up the area by raking the leaves and pine straw into a small pile. As I lit a fire to burn them, a breeze picked up from the east and spread the fire into the woods near McGirt's Creek. Fortunately, there were no roads, houses, or people in that area in those days.

On Saturdays, we spent a nickel to ride Jacksonville's Motor Transit Company Naval Air Station bus to town. The Navy bus station was on the corner of Adams and Clay Streets. We walked past the Times-Union building on Pearl Street, the George Washington Hotel on the corner of Julia Street, and Furchgott's on the Hogan Street corner. The Barnett Bank had a wire-photo news picture in their display window which was very interesting because we had no TV then. The only news we saw was either in the newspaper or in the movie theater with Movietone or Pathe newsreels. We'd select a movie theater by walking down Forsyth Street looking at the poster and snapshots displays at four theaters, The Empress, Imperial, Palace and Florida. We usually wound up at the Imperial that had the good cowboy movies: Gene Autry, Johnny Mack Brown, or Hop-a-long Cassidy. The Short Subject reels were always funny. I always looked forward to the Edgar Kennedy and the Three Stooges reels. The movies only cost 9 cents, and a box of popcorn was 10 cents.

Afterwards, we'd stop at the Krystal for a 5 cent Orange Crush and a 7 cent Krystal burger. Woolworth's Five and 10 Cents Store had entrances on Forsyth Street and Main Street. We usually went in on the Forsyth Street side because it was near the Toy Department. We'd exit on Main Street because The Kress Store was right next door with another opportunity to scan the toys. Two blocks away was the Burgess Battery Store which sold airplane kits and balsa wood. I would assemble an airplane almost every week and hang them on a string that ran across the top of my bedroom. I even constructed a model of the Wright Brothers first airplane, copying it from a photo of that historic flight.

At night following supper and finishing homework, I'd turn on my Silvertone (Sears) radio on my bedside table and listen to comedy shows like Jack Benny, Fred Allen, Baby Snooks, and Red Skelton. One of my favorite shows was "Can You Top This?" where three personalities, Senator Ford, Harry Hershfield, and Joe Laurie, Jr. each had to tell a joke funnier than one sent in by a listener. They were pretty good because their jokes had to be on the same subject as the one from the listener. I don't remember many sports programs, except the Joe Louis boxing matches, and Bill Stern's broadcast of the famous Army– Notre Dame football game. Army was ranked number 1 and Notre Dame number 2. The game ended a scoreless tie with neither team crossing the goal line. On Saturday nights, we'd listened to "Your Hit Parade", a program of the week's top ten tunes. This was when the teenager's heart-throb Frank Sinatra usually sang the week's top hit.

CHAPTER 07 - Trouble on the Home Front

I have mixed emotions about my home life. Being wartime, my mother drove the shuttle van at NAS Jacksonville. It made stops all around the base, and she occasionally drove it to Cecil Field, eleven miles to the west of the NAS. She planted a victory garden behind our house where I enjoyed picking and snacking on Cherry tomatoes and English peas. On Saturdays, she did the laundry on a GE washing machine. She placed a tubful of clean water beside it to rinse the items she passed through a wringer near the edge of the washer. My main chore was to vacuum and dust the house and to keep the front porch swept. My mother was very outgoing and loved to go to neighborhood parties. My brother and I had a few unpleasant memories of the evenings that she came quite tipsy.

My father was rather quiet and reserved and enjoyed his work at the Benjamin Lee Auxiliary Navy Base in Green Cove Springs. He car-pooled with a couple of co-workers since gasoline was rationed during the war. Edgar Clancy, an electrician, was one of the riders. One year for my birthday, Mr. Clancy gave me an electric motor. I was really excited because when I had a Lionel electric train a couple of years earlier, I disassembled it and raced the stripped "engine with wheels" around the tracks. When I looked at my new gift, I said, "Gee, I wish every day was my birthday!" Mother scolded me for saying that.

Mr. Clancy's wife, Margaret, was a good friend of my mother. When our neighbor, Mr. Dobbins, asked my mother if she'd like to go to California, she agreed after he explained that his company had a car that had to be delivered to the west coast. Mother and Mrs. Clancy drove the car that long distance, stopping at tourist sites along the way. That's when I first learned of the Carlsbad Caverns in New Mexico.

24

My father, like his father, was an excellent carpenter. One day I was surprised to see him building a rowboat. The frame was laid on top of two sawhorses in our backyard. He fastened the side boards to a block of wood for the bow with long screws that he counter-sunk and filled with something like putty or plastic wood. He separated the sides in the middle of the boat with boards and then with screw clamps bent the sides to a narrower boat stern. As he added the boards for the bottom of the boat, he placed a heavy string-like material between each board, apparently to allow for expansion or contraction or to maintain water tightness.

We launched the boat at McGirt's Creek, a branch of Ortega River and my brother and I often rowed it along the wooded shoreline. One day, we started to explore a narrow inlet. Suddenly, an alligator raised his head above the waterline in front of us. Almost frozen in fear, we slowly eased the oars to move the boat in reverse towards the open waters of the creek. A few days later, I took the boat to the Ortega River. The railroad bridge near Roosevelt Blvd. was so low we had to lay across the seat of the boat to clear the bottom of the bridge. I learned about the changing levels of the water while fishing from the dock on the west side of McGirt's Creek. Sometimes the water was only a foot below the dock at high tide, but as the tide went out my line went a couple of feet lower to reach the water.

When I was about 13 years old, a man named George Stich, who worked for the Jacksonville Gas Company, often came to our house. We soon learned that he and his wife had divorced, and after a year or so we saw him with mother nearly every day. My brother and I never liked his sharp tone with us and his bitter attitude with the outside world. Finally, out of frustration, my father left for New Jersey to stay with his father in Pine Beach. Occasionally, Mr. Stich would come to our house with either a bottle of Seagram 7 or Southern Comfort whiskey. When the bottle was empty, we never knew whether they wind up in an argument that led to a fight, or if they would party and turn up the phonograph real loud until 2 or 3 A.M.

Several weeks later, we learned that my father had a nervous breakdown and was admitted to a Sanitarium in New Jersey. When Mr. Stich and my mother heard this, they were furious and said he must come back to Jacksonville immediately. The next time I saw him, he looked at me with a glassy stare in his eyes. He just hugged me and hardly said anything.

CHAPTER 08 - Good Schools our Stability

My first school in Florida was Ortega Elementary on Baltic Avenue. At first, they thought I should enter the fourth grade because when we left New Jersey in April without finishing that school year.

ORTEGA ELEMENTARY SCHOOL

But my mother, having been an elementary school teacher in New Jersey, convinced them to place me in Mrs. Floyd's fifth-grade class. There she taught me a love of poetry by introducing me to "The Village Blacksmith." The next year I transferred to newly constructed Venetia Elementary. It was only seven blocks from home. There were a few occasions where I misjudged the walking time and was sent to the Principal's Office for being tardy. I got to know Mrs. Mott quite well. One of my favorite subjects was Social Studies. I enjoyed it so much that I finished reading the book long before my teacher, Mrs. Overstreet, had covered the first three chapters. I remember her also for her admonition, "There's a time and a place for everything." As I served on the School Boy Patrol, I would walk to the middle of Timuquana Road and hold up my Stop Sign so students could safely cross the road. In November, Patrol Boys from different parts of the city gathered downtown to join and march in the Armistice parade.

The next summer, my father drove us to Miami Road on Jacksonville's Southside. We went into a store where he bought my brother and me each a second-hand bicycle. I often rode it down to Timuquana Road to fish at McGirts Creek. With the line and cork floating in the glassy water, I would watch the towering cumulus clouds fill the sky as the temperature climbed into the 90's. When the clouds grew dark and threatening, I hopped on my bike and tried to beat the rain to our house. On a couple of occasions, I heard the large raindrops striking the pavement behind me as I turned up onto the driveway and into the garage with its open door.

One day I rode my bike about 23 miles way down Roosevelt Blvd, past Orange Park and through Green Cove Springs and onto State Road 16 to see my father at work at Lee Field. When I pedaled up to his workplace, he was really surprised as he saw me peddle through the wide doorway into his shop. He soon gave me a tour of the base and even took me to the "Link Trainer" building. The Link Trainer was a flight simulator which looked like a miniature plane. It had controls and instruments with a hood that could cover the cockpit to teach pilots orientation problems when flying in the dark or in clouds. If a pilot did not learn that, they could lose the true feeling between down and up which could cause them to fly into the ground when they felt like they were flying level.

On October 20, 1944, I was excited to hear on the radio that we would be having a tropical storm. Around 9 AM, the wind and rain started to increase. We soon discovered the rainwater was blowing into the house around the windows and under the kitchen door. All morning we did nothing but watch the rain, wipe the window sills and mop the floor. The weather bulletin on the radio said that the wind and rain would cease around noon when the center of the storm arrived. They said not to go outside during the calm because the other half would soon bring dangerous winds from the opposite direction. We waited for three hours and it still was calm outside. Finally, when a little breeze came up, we went outside and held up a sheet by the corners to feel the force of the wind. The second half of the storm was not as fierce as the first part. Afterwards, we learned that a power line had fallen across a car in Venetia. The driver was electrocuted when he stepped out of the car to remove the wire. For months afterward, we saw all of the young pine trees still leaning towards the southwest because of the strong northeast gales.

Boy Scout Troop 32 met at the Venetia Elementary School. I bought a Boy Scout handbook and some merit badge books and started earning enough badges to become a Life Scout, one step short of Eagle. One day, my father met with a few of us at the vacant lot where we often played softball. We decided to play court to learn courtroom procedure. I played the part of a lawyer about to obtain testimony from one of my friends. After telling him to raise his right hand, I said, "Do you swear to hell---". I was shocked and embarrassed at what I said, but all the boys laughed. I don't remember my father's reaction because I was too embarrassed to look at him.

We caught the city bus at the corner of Timuquana Road and Roosevelt Blvd. On the frigid winter mornings, we found shelter from the northerly wind against the wall of an ornamental stucco structure at the intersection of two sidewalks. It took only 10 minutes to reach Lake Shore Junior High School where I attended the seventh grade. The bus would turn off Roosevelt Blvd. onto Lake Shore Blvd, where I spotted the expanding Huckins Yacht Company, which was building PT boats for the U.S. Navy. One day we learned that a PBY Flying Boat Patrol plane had crashed near our bus route. The next day we passed the burned wreckage between the Black Jack oak trees not far from our school's playground. Lake Shore was a newly constructed a red brick two-story building on Bayview Road. I noticed the rafters in the ceiling of the large gym were constructed by heavy wood timbers because of the shortage of steel during the war. The playground had dry, powdery sand that was hotter than Jacksonville Beach when the scorching sun on the lengthening spring days grew longer.

Around the same year, my brother Richard who still attended Venetia Elementary School, saw two Grumman TBF Avengers collide overhead while he was on afternoon schoolboy patrol duty. The airplanes were heading west over Venetia in formation, preparing to turn left towards the airfield. But airplane # 2 peeled to the left prematurely. It struck plane #1 which hadn't peeled left, causing it to lose its right wing. Both pilots were killed as both aircraft crashed in the swamp south of Timuquana Road.

Among my favorite subjects in the 7th grade at Lake Shore Junior High School were algebra, mechanical drawing, and woodshop. My teachers, Virginia Wainwright and Mrs. Faulkner, steered me into these fields of science and graphics design. Learning to use a T-Square, a ruler, and triangles helped me in my career to design hurricane maps and graphs years later as a meteorologist at Channel 4. I used my woodworking knowledge to renovate four homes I later lived in. Also, I constructed office furniture for my Weather Office at WJXT where I originally had only a desk in the newsroom. When it was moved to half of an office across the hall that I shared with the camera equipment, built a bookcase for weather manuals, and an extension to my desk for clipboards and the weather instruments.

In school, I usually had no trouble with most subjects, including algebra and English. I loved Mrs. Godwin's Music class when we sang a lot of the good old times songs, and they were not just American classics. We learned the Mexican "La Cucaracha" and Australian "Waltzing Matilda", as well as the Scottish "My Bonnie Lies over the Ocean". One day, my science teacher Mr. Van Sise taught us about plant growth and photosynthesis. In a study of plant nutrients, he asked for volunteers to bring a cup of soil to discover the location of the most fertile soil. Since I lived near McGirts Creek, my sample caused the greatest growth of the beans that were planted.

When I reached the seventh grade, I occasionally rode my bike to school when it wasn't too hot or cold. There was so little traffic in those days that I had no trouble riding on Roosevelt Blvd; in fact, during the summer I would ride it all the way into the King Street Bicycle Shop for accessories and parts. I could remove the brake assembly, clean and oil it, and put it back together again. A year later, I had to replace the tires on both wheels. Unfortunately, I didn't tighten the front wheel securely. One Sunday morning I rode the bike down the Venetia sidewalk, and when I reached the curb at the end of the sidewalk, the front wheel came off! I landed on my right forehead and face, tearing the skin off. Hearing my cries, a neighbor across the street came to my aid. I was very appreciative of her care. I had to miss the last few weeks of the 8th grade until the huge scab across my face healed.

When I was in the ninth grade, my brother Richard came to Lake Shore in the seventh grade. After school when waiting to catch the city bus home, I loved to make paper airplanes and fly them towards the west wall of the school. The afternoon sun heated the wall and the rising thermals would carry the plane nearly up to the roof. One day

Richard and I were surprised to see Mr. Stich come toward us. When he got to us he led us towards the bicycle rack and told us, "Your father has died!" I was stunned and silent, but Richard cried. He explained to us that my father had placed a hose from our washing machine into the car's exhaust during the night, placed it in the car trunk, and climbed into it with the motor running. I remembered that we had slept late that morning and were late to the bus stop. Mother hurriedly got us in the car and caught up with the bus. As we boarded the bus, someone said there was a hose dragging behind that car! Our father was such a quiet, reserved, and conscientious man that had several close friends, but mother was very demanding, and frequently criticized him for not being as energetic as she; consequently, there was seldom any peace in our household. Richard and I thought our home was very disruptive when my father was in New Jersey and she and Mr. Stich could drink and party 'til all hours of the night, but after my father died and she married her lover, both Richard and I couldn't wait to grow up and leave home.

CHAPTER 09 - Moving into the City

After finishing Junior High School, I faced new adjustments. Our house in Venetia was sold, and we moved briefly into an apartment on Riverside Avenue before moving downtown. We lived upstairs in Dr. Gorman's two-story house at 615 Laura Street. We painted the walls, used a dishpan on a table for a sink, and bought a block of ice every 2 days for the Ice Box. The first winter we got a tin metal heater that had a stovepipe running to the fireplace which led to the chimney. On the coldest nights, Mr. Stich balled up sheets of newspaper for fuel and stuffed them into the stove. The paper ignited so rapidly that the entire stove turned red hot! For taking a bath, we had to light a gas burner for hot water. Across the street was Estes-Krause Funeral Home, which in those days also furnished ambulance service for the city. Occasionally the siren would sound as they answered an emergency call, pulling out of the driveway, and turning left onto Beaver Street. The wailing sound would fade away among the canyons of buildings in the city.

Living downtown was very convenient. We could walk to the movies on Saturday, and walk to First Baptist Church around the corner or Snyder Memorial Methodist Church a few blocks down Laura Street. This was three years before television came to Jacksonville, and radio provided much of our entertainment. One block away across the street was the Jacksonville Journal building, which housed the giant newspaper presses. Around noon on weekdays, newspaper carriers would head to street corners downtown, shouting news headlines to the passing pedestrians. Above the newspaper presses was radio station WJHP. The letters stood for John H. Perry, Publisher. It was there I met Speed Veal and Ted Chapeau, who called himself "Lazy-Bones" on the radio. Ted talked with a slow, southern drawl that fit the sleepy image of an old southern town. Around the corner was the broadcast studio of WPDQ in the basement of a First Baptist building. Their transmitter was located on Jacksonville's Westside under the tall antenna towers on Normandy Blvd.

While attending Robert E. Lee High School, I rode the city bus past 5 Points to McDuff Avenue where I got off to walk to school. I occasionally stopped at the Lee High shop to buy a pack of Champion notebook paper or some other school supply. My homeroom teacher was Leroy MacGowen, head of the Science Department. I loved most of the subjects taught by my teachers such as Hilda Brantley. Among them was history with Mrs. Winchester, who may have been part Native American because that was the part of history she emphasized. We also had to be aware of current events. I enjoyed my Geometry class with Mrs. Johnella Harden, except for Martha Williamson's desk being in front of mine. She always tried to get me to show her my answers when tests were given. I signed up for Physics in the 11th grade taught by Dorothy Thomas. I was having trouble with a full load and family problems and had to drop the class. I was taking Latin with Mrs. Rogers. It was fairly easy because of all my prior Spanish courses. In my senior year, I had no trouble with Physics, Chemistry, and Trigonometry. I never had problems with English. It was just the Literature part that was not my bag. I loved the poetry, but not Shakespeare.

The only part of Physical Education I liked was playing volleyball and running track. I never could understand basketball, the dribbles or double dribbles. I liked baseball and football but didn't have enough size or skill to participate. Study Hall helped me because I worked at the downtown St. Johns Theatre evenings, so I tried to get as much homework done in school so I didn't have much to do when I got home from work around 10:30 PM.

I made only 35 cents an hour working at the St. Johns Theater, but it gave me an experience about dealing with people. I also learned about show business since I'd watch the audience reactions to the movies, and I could study the acting techniques since I saw each movie seven or eight times. Each movie played either three or four days, or the popular ones would run a week or longer. I learned that one of the first movies at the St. Johns was "Yankee Doodle Dandy", the story of George M. Cohan, but the first long-running while I worked there was "My Wild Irish Rose" with Dennis Morgan and Arlene Dahl. There were more than a hundred patrons lined up on Forsyth Street waiting for the next performance. As ushers, we were sometimes assigned to be a "barker". We would stand outside the theater entrance and shout things like "The next complete show starts in 40 minutes" to attract customers. After most patrons were seated and fewer people needed to be lead to their seats, we would become "runners". We were given posters about upcoming movies that we "ran" to the many hotels in Jacksonville. At the time there were 12 or more. We ran into each one, sliding the posters into a movie display in their lobbies.

1949 Mr and Mrs George Stich
George's stepfather and mother

My stepfather, George Stich, was a man with many frustrations. Being a salesman for several local businesses, he always felt the pressure of having to close deals in the struggling post World War II economy. In addition, he occasionally experienced an epilepsy-like seizure that left him temporarily stiff and unconscious.

When faced with these problems, he turned to Seagram's 7 or Southern Comfort. During evenings when he came home with the brown bag containing a "fifth", which is 4/5 of a quart or one-fifth of a gallon, of liquor. After my brother and I went to sleep, we would be awakened by loud music with Mr. Stich singing and my mother crying.

He would shout at her and follow up by slapping her to become quiet.

My brother and I would lie in bed praying that they would stop and fall asleep. Fortunately, the fighting was never directed at us. Occasionally the police were called by neighbors between midnight and 3 AM and we could get about 3 or 4 hours sleep before having to get up for school.

Fortunately, I had a few close friends at school and where I worked at the theater. Being one of seven or eight ushers, we learned how to serve or deal with theater patrons. And viewing many repeats of various movies, we felt that we became acquainted with the various characters portrayed in the movies. To convince the public to see the latest movie, various techniques were used. The most eye-catching one was the gluing of a 3x8 foot poster to the sidewalk in front of the theater with a few coats of shellac or varnish to protect it from foot traffic. Also, we also had large illuminated posters in the lobby. I especially remember one Friday night when a teenage couple spotted one. The poster had a picture of a sad young woman under huge letters that said, NOT WANTED". As the doorman took their tickets, the girl made a connection with the picture, and dashed up to it saying, "That's me!" But she quickly turned away when she read the subtitle, "The Story of an Unwed Mother".

There was a button on the wall near the aisles leading to the seats that connected to the projection booth. There were certain numbers of buzzes that informed the projection booth if the sound of the movie was too soft, or too loud. The head usher could alert the operator to correct the problem. When seats were hard to find during a very popular movie, the only ones available were on the very front row, or on the extreme sides. As we showed patrons were shown to these seats, they often refused to sit there. We tried to encourage by telling them that they could sit there until they spot someone leaving farther back so they could switch to those seats. These were the days that moviegoers would often enter the theater in the middle of the movie, and then leave in the next showing when the part they had seen came up.

The St. Johns Theater had a lovely lounge area on the mezzanine. There was a large mural of a blooming Magnolia Tree on the wall by the staircase leading up to it. On one occasion, a couple of sparrows flew in the front door of the theater that tried to find the way out. They made several attempts to land on the branches of the mural, failing to catch hold. The mezzanine had several doors surrounding it. One door led to the ladies room, others to a telephone, a men's room, and the last one the Manager's office. With Jacksonville being a Navy town, I quickly learned some of the Navy lingo. A sailor came to me and asked directions to the "head". I showed him the Manager's door. I quickly learned that the Navy called the Rest Room a head!

Some movies were so bad that the theater was nearly empty. Such was the case of "Beyond the Forest" starring Bette Davis. Most of the ushers were released for the evening, including me and my friend, Jimmy Taylor, who lived on Duval Street, not far from the Gator Bowl. It was Friday night and the lights were on at the Gator Bowl. Since we usually worked Friday nights, we realized that this was our chance to see the last half of the high school football game. We had no tickets, but then there was no one at the gate to take a ticket, so we just walked right in and watch all of the last quarter. We hadn't missed much because Lee was playing Landon, and the final score was 0 - 0. I not only worked downtown, but I found many things to do there, too. Some stores had pinball machines that could award me free games. I played long after the five nickels I got for my quarter were gone. I enjoyed reading, so I could easily walk to the Public Library on Adams Street where there were many magazines, such as Life, Look, Popular Science, Popular Mechanics, Colliers, Coronet, and Readers Digest. I would check out required reading for Book Reports. With no television, at home we listened to radio programs or music played by DJ's (disk jockeys) Popular songs were performed by orchestras like Tommy Dorsey, Spike Jones, Harry James, and Guy Lombardo's Royal Canadians. We played the phonograph. As long as I could remember, we listened to music recorded on large, brittle 78 RPM records until the smaller vinyl 45's came out in 1949. Around that time, there was a musician's union strike when no instrumental music was legally recorded. A group called the Harmonicats made recordings about that time because they did not belong to the union. One of their best songs was "Peg of my Heart". After the strike, one of the first recordings was Les Paul and Mary Ford's "How High the Moon" and "Mockingbird Hill".

CHAPTER 10 - Almost Homeless

In 1948, my brother Richard and I left our Laura Street home to visit our grandparents in New Jersey. Uncle Clinton took us clamming in Barnegat Bay. To find the clams, pieces of canvas were sowed over our feet so we could feel them in the mud on the bottom of the bay. After we collected several bushels, we spent the time riding back to the dock sorting the different sizes of clams.

Mother had always told me that Uncle Clinton liked Richard more than me and that he wanted him to stay with him. That made me very uncomfortable as we stayed at my grandmother, Mamie Cranmer's, house in Mayetta. I wanted to return to Jacksonville.

Instead of telling them my wishes, I left a note of my wishes on the family Bible, walked across the fields behind the house to highway US 9. I caught the bus to Toms River and got off at Pine Beach at my grandfather, George Winterling's, house on Grant Avenue. He lived there with his second wife, formerly Emma Stoldt. He taught me how to finish sheetrock walls by applying tape joint compound. After two weeks, I earned enough money purchase a Greyhound ticket back to Jacksonville.

Arriving in Jacksonville, I discovered mother and Mr. Stich had moved to the Jefferson Hotel on Adams Street, near Lee Street. It was summer and because of acne breaking out on my face, I went into the bathroom to heat washcloths with hot water. I placed the steaming washcloths over my face. Around five minutes later, I would then place Noxzema on the skin for the night. I guess it helped dry the pimples.

With my brother Richard still in New Jersey, my mother would start crying for him as the radio played the song, "Blue Bird of Happiness", which only added more to her grief.

Head Usher and Student Manager St. Johns Theater

My happiness came from my job at the St. Johns Theater. The smash hit movie, "Romance on the High Seas" with Doris Day had been playing for 4 weeks. The theater was still having large crowds because there was no television in Jacksonville. Business was so good that the theater manager, Sheldon Mandell, promoted me to Student Manager. I was taught how to count the day's cash income, report it to an owner in New York, and place it in the safe until depositing it at the nearby Atlantic National Bank the next day. Working this position, I often worked until the end of the last movie around Midnight. I remain thankful for all Mr. Mandell taught me about the world of business.

On August 27, 1949, a strong hurricane came up the Florida peninsula. It passed west of Jacksonville over Lake City as a tropical storm, but in Jacksonville our winds gusted as high as 85 mph, blowing down large signs, breaking store windows, and causing much tree and roof damage around the city. When school started in September, we moved from the Jefferson Hotel to the Floridian Hotel at the corner of Forsyth and Clay Streets. Around this time, the bicycle I had ridden for over 5 years was stolen from the Western Union office on Forsyth Street across from the theater. When I told Mr. Stich about this, he accused me of selling it! I couldn't believe he didn't believe me. A few weeks later, we had to sneak out of the hotel without paying our bill. All of our family possessions were left behind. What I missed most were the movies my father had taken of Richard and me in New Jersey. He took pictures from the days Richard was 2 years old and I was five. We had movies of visiting the 1939 New York World Fair in New York City.

We stayed a few weeks in an apartment on Adams Street near Broad until mother got a job managing a rooming house at 617 Hogan Street, ironically the site of the future home of the Ruth Lindsay auditorium of the First Baptist Church. I would occasionally sweep and mop the floors. On the north side of Beaver Street was a Radio-Television school, training a new generation of technicians for TV. This was before most homes had TV sets. Television finally came to Jacksonville on September 15, 1949. WMBR-Channel 4, the forerunner of WJXT, inaugurated a display of this new medium in the newly renovated Cohen Brothers Department Store. This was the first building in Jacksonville to install escalators, which ran from the basement to the third floor. Since this was only 2 blocks from where I lived, I rode the escalator to the Mezzanine where I saw the cameras and TV Station employees transmit pictures to television monitors placed around the store. Little did I know that I would devote more than fifty years to this venture with that very same station. In those days there were few TV sets in homes. People would gather on the sidewalk to watch the pictures in store windows, like Radio Center next to the Arcade Theater on Forsyth Street. In the neighborhoods, you could tell who was watching television, especially on Friday nights. Interior lighting would flicker through the windows where a TV was displaying shows like the Pabst Blue Ribbon Friday night fights.

Our high school graduation ceremony took place at the George Washington Hotel. We had to dress formal, but I didn't own a pair of black shoes. So I bought a bottle of Griffin Liquid Black Shoe polish and dyed my brown shoes black. After graduation, mother and Mr. Stich moved to a few places near 5 Points, and I rented a room at 129 West Beaver Street. It was very convenient because as Student Manager, I spent many hours working at the theater. There were many restaurants downtown, but the most economical were Hargraves at State and Main Streets, the Athens on Main Street, the 324 Restaurant on Forsyth Street. Among my favorite dishes were Salisbury Steak and breaded Veal Cutlets. The Athens Restaurant had the best Greek Salad and Spaghetti dinners. Aside from the Krystal and Milligan Hamburgers, my favorite was from Amber House, which was on Forsyth Street across from the St Johns Theater. But my most economical meals would be a can of Chung King Chop Suey heated on a hot plate in my room.

In February 1950, I decided to turn my life in the direction of my interest in aviation. I first went to the Navy Recruiting Office in the Post Office Building on Monroe Street. When I expressed my interest in flying, they said I needed to have two years of college. I then went down the hall to the Air Force Recruiter who encouraged me to enlist and then apply for Cadet training. When I signed up, they said I would receive orders to go to Lakeland Air Force Base in San Antonio, TX for Basic training. When I informed my boss, Sheldon Mandell, of my decision, he took me into his office, gave me my week's salary, and said "goodbye". I guess if I had told him that I had been drafted, he would have been more cordial.

CHAPTER 11 - A Home in the Air Force

With the exception of a family visit to Ohio in 1935, this was my first trip west of the Atlantic seaboard. I had traveled north to New Jersey via Philadelphia on the Atlantic Coast Railroad's Champion twice since moving to Florida in 1941. Now at the age of 18, I found myself a young man heading west! At first, the trip seemed no different as we rolled through Tallahassee. But as the train rolled in the evening darkness, a porter led me to a Pullman bunk bed. What a delight! On my previous nocturnal train rides, I had to sleep upright in a coach seat.

I awoke the next morning as the train was approaching Louisiana and New Orleans. I had just enough time between trains to tour the incredibly wide Canal Street before catching the Sunset Limited to San Antonio. It was well after dark when a truck from Lackland Air Force Base picked us up at the train station and took us to the Induction Center at the base.

As I recall, we all had our head shaved and an issue of clothes. I can't remember if we got our shots at that time or on one of the following days. I was given a serial number AF 14-353-043 and assigned to Squadron 3724, Flight 4883. We were then taken to our barracks just before 3 AM. We were rudely awakened around 6 AM to stand formation and then marched to the Mess Hall for breakfast.

1950 Basic training in the USAF was rough, but I felt that it was good for me

Our first drill sergeant was a short corporal who gave orders sharply. He always expected perfection from each of us in everything we did. For our first inspection, we stood at attention in our stiff starched khaki uniforms and polished shoes and belt buckles. I stared straight ahead as I heard the corporal finding something wrong with almost every man he inspected.

Thinking I had prepared myself perfectly, I felt confident when he stepped in front of me. He looked me up and down, and suddenly I heard a ripping sound as he snatched the flaps on my shirt pockets. I thought he had ripped them off! With my heart beating rapidly, I heard him say, "Next time, make sure you button these flaps!"

During the next few days, we attended classes that showed films about military procedures, and health care that included venereal disease and gonorrhea. This was important because of the risk of being enticed by girls outside the base attracted by our uniform (and looks). We were given a card with our General Orders, which we had to memorize. When we were assigned guard duty, we were required to know them and to respond with the correct order when asked to.

One night I was assigned to guard the Officers Club between 10 PM and 2 AM. The night was pitch-black, and the air was filled with the eerie distant sound of the song "Harbor Lights". Those were four long hours, and we were eager to get back to our barracks around 3 AM. We were only asleep about 2 hours when the lights came on in the barracks and we were told to get dressed in our fatigues to pull "KP". That's Kitchen Police where we worked in the Mess Hall, setting up the food line, the condiments on the tables, and a lot of other things like mopping the floors, emptying garbage cans, and then peeling potatoes for the next meal. If we were lucky, we got to eat an ice cream bar between meals. It seemed like an endless day until we could finally mop the floors and turn out the lights around 8 PM.

1950 George after 7 weeks of basic training on leave in San Antonio, TX

We had inspections when an officer entered the barracks and we had to stand at attention. Our beds had to be tightly made, so tight that a quarter would bounce if it was tossed on the blanket. Our clothes had to be orderly hung on hangers behind our bed, and our towels and underwear had to be "rolled securely" in our footlockers at the foot of the bed. We went 8 weeks before we got a pass to go into San Antonio. I got a picture of myself for 25 cents in a photo booth that frightened my mother. Because of my military training, I posed rigidly with a stern stare at the camera for the picture.

As the end of my basic training drew near, I was given an aptitude test to determine what trade school I would be assigned to. On a scale of one to 10, I scored a 9 on all but two categories. I was then shown a list of career paths. The one that attracted me most was Weather. There was much I wanted to learn about weather because meteorology and weather were not taught in the '40s when I was in school. All I knew about weather forecasts was the word on the front page of the newspaper, the weather report on the radio, or from my weather experiences outdoors. I observed the wind and rain with two tropical storms, one in 1944 that passed through Jacksonville, and the second one in 1949 that passed well west of the city, but shattered several store windows in downtown Jacksonville. Fortunately, my next assignment would be to enroll in the USAF Weather Observers School at Chanute Field, Illinois.

CHAPTER 12 - Starting in Meteorology

I had a two week leave to spend back to Jacksonville. I spent most of that time with my girlfriend, sometimes waiting for her to get off work at the concession stand in the St Johns Theater, then walking with her from the downtown theater on Forsyth Street through Confederate Park to Walnut Street. She lived with her parents in a house on Walnut Court. With no TV, we often would walk and talk around her neighborhood. Once I visited a Youth for Christ meeting at Berea Baptist Church on Phoenix Avenue. One evening, we were sitting in the swing on her front porch when we heard on the radio that North Korea had attacked South Korea. That was on June 25, 1950, the beginning of the Korean War. We wondered what effect that would have on the 3½ years I had left on my enlistment.

I soon left for Rantoul, Illinois, and Chanute Air Force Base. It was there that I met Jack Hall from Palo Alto, California. He, like me, loved the outdoors and we became good friends. To keep up with the news from Jacksonville, I had subscribed to the Florida Times-Union, my hometown newspaper. While at Chanute, I learned that two tropical storms hit Jacksonville, one in September that dumped over 10 inches of rain, and a second one that passed west of the city delivered wind gusts up to 85 mph.

One Sunday morning, I decided to visit a church in the town of Rantoul. Before then, I had only attended chapel services on the base. I didn't know where the Baptist church was, but while looking around I spotted a Nazarene church. I had never been in one of that denomination before, so I walked in just as the service was beginning. After we had sung a few familiar hymns, the pastor asked us to stand for prayer. As soon as I bowed my head and closed my eyes, I was surprised to hear nearly everyone in the building praying aloud at the same time. Many stayed in their pews, but a several were walking and praying around the pews and in the aisles. I didn't know if this was just a denominational thing or a regional practice, but it left a lasting impression of a different form of church prayers from this church in Illinois.

While waiting a few weeks for the next weather class, I was assigned to various duties on the base. In addition to loading trucks and performing KP duty, I also received a certificate for learning how to stoke the coal furnace in our barracks. Finally, I joined the Weather Observers class, conducted by Sergeant Phillips. He taught the four groups of clouds – low, middle, high, and vertical development, and the various kinds of weather instruments. I learned about the gas in weather balloons. I wrote a letter to my high school science teacher, Dorothy Thomas, about the process of making hydrogen by depositing zinc pellets into a cylinder containing hydrochloric acid, similar to an experiment we had done in her Chemistry class at Lee High School.

It was interesting learning how the maximum and the minimum thermometer worked, and the requirements for locating the equipment in an instrument shelter to keep them from giving false readings in the bright sun or the nocturnal heat loss by radiation under clear skies. We learned the proper location for the rain gauge, and how to read the water level in the collection tube. Upon completion of the course, I was given a certificate stating that I had finished at the top of my class.

While at Chanute, we occasionally assembled on the tarmac between the hangars and the runways. With a few of my favorite planes, the F86 Sabrejet parked nearby, we'd march by a reviewing stand where base officers stood. Finally, I was most inspired by the evening that our classes assembled outside the front entrance of the base. As the sun was sinking, and the sky turned from dark blue to reddish orange, we heard the sound of a bugler playing "Taps" on the loudspeakers. In the silence that followed the last notes of "taps," we marched into darkness back to our barracks on Chanute Air Force Base.

CHAPTER 13 - First Job in a Weather Station

1951 George arrives at Turner Field, Albany GA weather station

My next assignment was at Turner Air Force Base, Albany, Georgia. Turner Field was a SAC (Strategic Air Command) base under the command of General Curtis LeMay. Since we were now at war, tall barbed-wire fences were being installed around the base and guards were stationed in towers around the field. For night patrol duty, the guards wore leather suits, the insides lined with wool. This was the beginning of jet aviation era. The first jets we saw were F-80 Shooting Stars. One problem of the early jet technology was the problem of flame-outs. I saw one F-80 approaching the field when his engine suddenly quit. The powerless plane made a pancake landing short of the runway, its wheels flying off on impact. Fortunately, there was no fire and he escaped with no serious injury.

Operating a weather station meant that we all worked shifts, day and night, seven days a week. Fortunately, we worked 7 days on and 4 days off. This allowed me time to walk to the US 82 Highway and hitchhike to Jacksonville. I got to meet many south Georgia locals on my rides and learned about towns like Sylvester, Tyty, Tifton, Alapaha, Willacoochee, Pearson, and Waycross. One day I rode in a car when the driver turned to the left east of Tifton away from US 82. Knowing that this was not the way to Waycross, I reminded him that I was going to Jacksonville. He said he was going to Jacksonville, too. I then learned that he was going to Jacksonville, Georgia!

Getting off at midnight, I often caught rides that let me out in the dark of night at a crossroad in the middle of nowhere. One time I heard a rustling sound in the trees approaching me, soon to learn that it was the only the rainy remnant of an evening thunderstorm. Most drivers in those days respected men in service uniforms because many were veterans from World War II. But one man driving me back to the base from Jacksonville was too friendly. He wanted me to spend the night with him in Albany. As we neared the road leading to Turner Field, I told him to let me out there because I had to report for duty at midnight.

Occasionally on my days off, I rode the city bus into Albany to see a movie or visit a few stores. On Sundays when I was not working, I attended the First Baptist Church. One summer day I went swimming at Radium Springs. The water was refreshingly cool. Suddenly, I noticed that I was the only one in the water. I discovered that everyone was looking at a water moccasin swimming at the far end of the spring. Wow! I didn't go there anymore after that experience.

One dark night around midnight in Jacksonville, I was walking down College Street by Riverside Park. As I headed towards Dellwood Avenue, the stars in the black sky appeared so near and bright that I felt like I could touch them. I suddenly felt the presence of God, and I asked Him what He wanted me to do. I felt that He told me to join the church and that I would find Him there. The next Sunday, I walked forward to the invitation at the end of the worship service at the First Baptist Church in Albany, Georgia. I told the pastor that I was accepting Jesus as Lord of my life. The following Sunday I was baptized by the Pastor Dr. Leonard Stephens. Through Bible study and attending Sunday School, I learned more about the Jesus way of living. From that day forward, I always prayed for His will in decisions that affected my life.

As Weather Observer at Turner Field, I read the weather instruments and logged the readings on a form called WBAN. The letters stand for Weather-Bureau-Army-Navy which was the official record of the weather for that day. I would then go to a teletype machine and type the coded report onto a strip of ticker tape. I would place the tape onto a box that would transmit it through a telephone line to a weather center when the weather center transmitted Turner Field's call letters, TRF. We had 8 different weather observers to cover 24 hours, 7 days a week. Everyone received a score at the end of the month based on the accuracy of their reports. Computation and entry errors were called discrepancies. Having been an excellent math and science student in High school, my score was often around 98%.

I enjoyed talking about the weather with our forecasters. Lt. Clark taught me a lot about forecasting and meteorology. We also had one of the first radars used at weather stations. It was an AN/APQ-13 radar developed by Bell Laboratories for B-29s in the Pacific during the war. Often when I saw distant lightning at night, I would turn on the radar and try to detect the rain by rotating the antenna and adjusting the tuning. One night I picked up a thunderstorm and discovered it was over Fitzgerald, Georgia while we had a clear, starry night in Albany.

CHAPTER 14 - College Life in Oklahoma

One day, Captain Marvin Lutz, who was in charge of the weather station, called me into his office for a review. He told me that I was rated "excellent", and that he was recommending me to a new meteorology program at Oklahoma A&M College, now Oklahoma State University. The Air Force assembled professors from schools like UCLA, the University of Chicago, New York University, and Massachusetts Institute of Technology. The course was called the Intermediate Meteorology School. Classes included climatology, map analysis, and meteorology. Each of us was taught math at a level higher than our high school education. I received 30 semester hours of college credit, plus 3 additional hours credit for a Synoptic Meteorology course I took at Oklahoma A&M College.

It was in the fall of 1951 that I saw snow for the first time since my childhood in New Jersey as I rode the Trailways bus into Oklahoma. It was just a few patches along the roadside near Tulsa. When I arrived in Stillwater, I was dazzled by a large red brick dormitory that was to be my home for the next eight months.

1951 At Oklahoma A&M Meteorology School

The building, called Bennett Hall, was a whole block long on the northern edge of the campus, right across the street from the Basketball Arena and Football Stadium. Our classes met inside the stadium under the seats.

One day I thought someone seated at the desk behind me was kicking my chair, but I soon learned that it was tremors from a minor earthquake.

For our Climatology class, each of us had to study the climate of various parts of the earth. My report was on South America, which contained many different climates. I learned about its topography, the seasons, and differences between the rain forests, the equatorial doldrums, and the intrusions of polar air from the south into Paraguay, Uruguay, and Brazil. I was impressed with Professor Rollo Dean's demonstration of streamline analysis. He could place wind reports on the chalkboard and then draw curving lines of wind flow that converged inward to cyclones (lows) and diverged outward from anticyclones (highs).

I renewed my friendship with Jack Hall, whom I first met at Chanute Field in 1950. We attended the First Baptist Church in Stillwater. A new sanctuary had just been dedicated with a beautiful stained-glass window on the wall behind the balcony. Above the choir, a lattice had been constructed in front of the organ pipes or speakers. I spent one Saturday helping students stapling a cheese-cloth curtain to it that could be illuminated by colored lights. On Sundays, Jack and his friend, Marvin Henry, and I attended a Sunday School class, following which we listened to inspiring sermons

45

delivered by the pastor, Sidney Maddox. During the week, I met many new friends at the Baptist Student Union which was located near the college campus. It was directed Reverend Kermit Whitaker, a man who had a warm, magnetic personality. Some of the students and I would meet on Sunday afternoons and visit the city jail and nursing homes. We ministered to many elderly and ailing people. My heart especially went out for those who were severely crippled with arthritis. We sang songs like Mansion over the Hilltop, A Closer Walk with Thee, Just a Little Talk with Jesus.

Although I didn't visit towns outside of Stillwater, I felt I learned much about the lives of Oklahomans from my friends in Stillwater. At the BSU, vesper services were held each evening around 6 PM where different students would give inspiring devotionals or tell their life experiences. We had many joyous times singing choruses, ones being sung at Youth for Christ meetings at that time. I began to teach myself to play hymns on the piano where we met for Vespers. One of my first was "When I Survey the Wondrous Cross" because it was easiest to learn and I loved the melody.

During the Christmas break, I caught a ride with a couple of students who were driving to Florida. I was really impressed with the rolling hills of northern Arkansas and the floodplain of the Mississippi River as we entered Mississippi at historic Vicksburg. When I was visiting mother at the Matthews' apartment on Dellwood Avenue, my stepfather, George Stich gave me a $20 bill and told me to buy a half pint of Seagram's 7 liquor in Five Points. I didn't like that because it reminded me of all the drunken binges he went on with my mother during my teen years.

When I visited my girlfriend, June, I realized that I no longer had the same feelings for her that I did before entering the service. I was eager to head back to school in Oklahoma. A fellow classmate, Richard Hoopes, picked me up in his small MG sports car. Since it was such a long drive, he decided to spend the night at the Duval Hotel on Monroe Street in Tallahassee. The next morning we made good time to Mobile as he was going around 70 mph, but when we hit US 90 in Mississippi which ran along the Gulf of Mexico we could see nothing but fog in front of the car. Nevertheless, he still drove close to 60 mph, until two headlights were coming straight for us. In the blink of an eye, he swerved the MG across the approaching lane onto the opposite shoulder. This is the same stretch of road that the blonde movie star Jayne Mansfield was decapitated when it slammed into a tractor-trailer that was halted by a mosquito spraying truck. Miraculously, we made it safely to New Orleans in one piece!

46

From New Orleans, I hitchhiked through Baton Rouge and at 2 AM was let out at a fork in the road because my driver was headed a different way. A half-hour later, a man driving a brand new 1951 Studebaker picked me up. He said that he was very tired and he wanted to grab an hour or two of sleep. He asked me to drive, and even though I had no drivers license, I welcomed the opportunity to drive this nice car all the way to Shreveport. From Shreveport, I caught a ride to Dallas, and from Dallas, I caught a ride all the way to Stillwater.

In 1951, my brother, Richard, also joined the Air Force. Being station at Henley Field near Dallas, he visited me in Stillwater and we had a good time catching up on each other's lives. Being two years younger than me, he often had a different group of friends. He also wound up being assigned to the opposite side of the globe, Germany, when I finally had duty in Alaska and the Aleutians. This was before computers and e-mails, and phoning long distance was expensive, so most of our communication was in detailed letters. Fortunately, I still have a few letters to remind me of things in our lives that I had been long forgotten. It was around this time that I finally wrote a "Dear John" letter to my former girlfriend, June, in Jacksonville. Like many high school romances, life's circumstances led us in different directions and we were only having a relationship that consisted of fading memories.

I never saw a tornado during my 8 months in Oklahoma. When I first arrived, I was told that a big hailstorm had shattered many of the roof tiles a few years earlier. At Stillwater, I gave my first blood donation and appeared on the radio for the first time pledging my support for the Red Cross appeal. Each morning when Reveille sounded in Bennett Hall, we jumped into our fatigues. It was often very breezy as we headed out the door and lined up for roll call. The most unusual thing was the temperature and wind were different almost every day. One day was very cold with a north wind, and other days it was quite mild with a south wind. I could see why weather was such a big thing there.

On the first floor of Bennett Hall was a serving line for our meals, and there was a lounge area for relaxing and reading. In the corner, there was a place to watch TV. That provided me with a unique experience to see weather broadcasts for the first time. The station was Channel 4, WKY TV. The news was broadcast by John Cameron Swayze. My first experience of watching television was when I visited my Uncle Clinton Cranmer in Clifton, New Jersey. He had a Dumont television in his apartment, and in the evening we walked by the storefronts in town where people gathered to watch wrestling matches. I later learned that my uncle married Eleanor Klazen, who had worked for Dumont around that time. On August 29, 1952, I graduated in second place from the top of my class of ninety students. I learned that I was assigned to the 7th Weather Group under the Alaskan Air Command at Elmendorf Air Force Base in Anchorage, Alaska.

CHAPTER 15 - Briefly Home, then Westward Ho!

My brother, Richard, was home on leave in Jacksonville, so I decided to spend a few days there with him before checking out at Stillwater. I hitchhiked to Tinker Field in Oklahoma City to catch a "hop" on a MATS, Military Air Transport Command) plane. Tinker Field had become recognized for the work of two forecasters, Lt. Col Ernest J. Fawbush and Colonel Robert C. Miller, who were pioneers in the technique of tornado forecasting. I finally caught a flight to Smyrna Air Force Base, outside of Nashville, Tennessee. I spent a chilly night in the wooden, unheated Operations Building wearing nothing but my summer khakis. All I could do was cover myself with newspapers and shiver, waiting for the sun to come up.

Finally, as the warm orange sunlight illuminated the base, I walked through the gates to US Highway 41, hoisted my right thumb and hitchhiked to Chattanooga and Atlanta, and after a visit to a gas station for a Coke and a package of Lance Peanut Butter Crackers resumed hitchhiking to Waycross and Jacksonville. Richard and I went downtown to visit my former workplace, the St. Johns Theater. We talked with the manager on duty and a few employees that we had known. I also contacted a former usher with me who had joined the Marines. His name was Woo Fang Yee, and he told me that he had spent a year in Korea. He said he was in North Korea when the Red Chinese soldiers swarmed across the Yalu River, catching the U.S. troops by surprise. He managed to find places to hide and make his way back to the remainder of his unit that had retreated into South Korea.

1952 Brothers home for Christmas

A few days later, Richard and I hitchhiked to Turner Field in Albany, Georgia. It took only took four rides and six hours to travel the distance of nearly 200 miles. We went to Base Operations and learned we both missed a plane that was going to Barksdale Air Force Base in Shreveport, Louisiana. We had to wait until the next day for a plane that was going Bergstrom Air Force Base in Austin, Texas. We ate a good meal at the base (hamburger, potatoes, huckleberry pie and ice cream), then rode the bus into town where Richard went to a movie, and I went to prayer meeting at the First Baptist to tell a few of my friends about my assignment in Alaska. The next morning we boarded a C-47 and had a very bumpy flight that lasted about 4 hours. After riding into town and eating a veal cutlet dinner, we caught a bus to Dallas where I spent the night with Richard at Hensley Field.

The next morning I caught a flight to Oklahoma City and then hitchhiked to Stillwater. I talked with a friend who told me his landlady had a vacant apartment. He said she would not charge me, but when I left I thanked her and gave her 20 dollars. I got to see a lot of my friends who were back from their summer break. When I told them I would be leaving for an assignment in Alaska, they had a nice party for me the next evening. On Wednesday, a bunch of us went to prayer meeting after the 6 PM vespers at the BSU. The following days, I helped the kids prepare for the annual BSU carnival. They asked me to go singing with them for the old people on Sunday, telling me that they had twenty carloads of kids the previous Sunday. The day ended with an unforgettable fellowship gathering after church that evening

Even though I was excited about the new experiences ahead for me in Alaska, I was sad that I might never see these friends again. When I told them that I was catching a 2 AM bus to California, I was very surprised when one of my friends, John Nance, offered to get up at that hour to drive me to the bus station. I waited an hour and there was no bus. When it finally arrived, the driver told me that the ticket agent had given me the wrong time…probably the time it left Tulsa. I felt very sorry that my friend had to get up so early in the morning for me to catch that bus. I had a three and a half hour wait between buses in Oklahoma City, so I went to see a boy I knew in the hospital there with a bone infection. Boy! He was really surprised to see me. As I talked with him, my pastor from the church in Stillwater suddenly walked in. He was very surprised to see me there. A couple hours passed before I headed back to the bus station.

From Oklahoma City, I rode the bus across the panhandle where I finally saw a mountain in the distance that was so far away that it took hours to reach. We were traveling on US Route 66 past Amarillo up to Santa Fe, New Mexico and not far from the Grand Canyon through Flagstaff, Arizona and the mountains were beautiful. The sun was low, and the shadowy effect on the mountains produced many different colors. I really wished I had a color camera to take pictures! We finally reached Los Angeles and transferred to another bus that took us through Bakersfield and the San Joaquin Valley. The countryside appeared so bountiful with orange trees, olive trees, cotton fields, grape arbors and all kinds of farm products like tomatoes and watermelons. I finally arrived in Pittsburg, California. I checked in around 5:45 PM, six hours before my deadline. I was glad I had taken extra time to stay with my friends in Stillwater.

At Camp Stoneman, I was to be processed for travel to Alaska, but it would be a week or more before they'd get to me because my name was near the bottom of the alphabet. In the meantime, I was assigned a few duties, like serving gravy on the chow line and passing out letters in the mail room. After processing was completed, we were bused to very long lines at the docks. After reaching the ferry, we lifted our large duffle bags to our shoulders and climbed the gangplank onto the vessel. It took us to Camp Mason, which was on the San Francisco Bay waterfront near the Golden Gate Bridge. It was there that we transferred to a World War II Liberty ship, the USNS Aiken Victory.

CHAPTER 16 - North to Alaska

1952 Sailing rough seas to Alaska

After sailing under the Golden Gate Bridge, we were served supper on a metal tray and found a place to sit on a bench on the sides of a long table that ran from bow to stern. As the ship left the bay, it encountered strong ocean ground swells that suddenly tipped the table up on one end and down on the other. Those who unfortunately sat on the lower end found themselves under a cascade of food and trays that had spilled onto them. That night, we were rocked to sleep in one of a series of stacked bunks below deck. The next morning, I was greeted by a misty view of Seattle. The ship only stopped for a short time. We were soon headed for the Gulf of Alaska.

On the open sea, the large ocean swells were spectacular. I watched how the bow of the ship sliced into the deep blue Pacific waters, creating a light blue outward moving wake. At night, I watched the glow of bright yellowish green particles of phosphorus in the water. By day, the blue sky was decorated with white cumulus clouds, some of them towering enough to create a curtain of white snow pellets that fell into the ocean. The ocean waves rocked the ship incessantly from side to side for two days. Some of us fought seasickness, hanging onto the rail, and a few heaved their meals overboard. I found that I could reduce the motion sickness by looking at each large wave approaching the ship, and by pulling and pushing on the rail I felt like I was rocking the ship. One of my friends stayed in his bunk for two days, unable to keep any food in his stomach.

On the morning of the fourth day, I awoke to notice that the ship was not rocking. I eagerly jumped off of my bunk and climbed the ladder up to the main deck. I saw that the ship was on glassy smooth waters cruising slowly past the massive rock islands of the Passage Canal.

1952 George arrives in Anchorage Alaska

Soon we docked at Whittier, Alaska and boarded a beautiful blue and yellow train. As the train pulled out, we could see the front half of the train as it ran on the winding tracks. Looking to the right through large windows, we were dazzled by the brilliantly white snow-covered mountains with a background of vivid blue skies.

Occasionally, we passed a few greenish colored glaciers, frozen rivers that were trapped between the mountains. The train went only about 30 mph, but it helped us take in all the majestic scenery.

When I got off the train and set foot on terra firma, it didn't feel so firm because I still felt the rocking sensation as if I were still on the ship. In fact, it took three days for my mind to stabilize that feeling. Anchorage was a small town with only two or three tall five to ten story buildings. The rest of it consisted of small buildings. Most were just bungalows but were also some very modern homes.

A nice highway followed the railroad where I saw everything from new Fords and Cadillacs to dump trucks. I liked the music on the radio stations in Anchorage. They were playing songs like "Pistol-Packin' Mama", "Don't Fence Me In" and "Cool, Cool, Cool of the Evening". I heard on the news that Eisenhower had won the election against

Adlai Stevenson for President. I wrote home that I liked "Ike" and that I thought he would be the best man for the country.

Hamburgers here cost 50 cents and dinners around $2.00 to $2.50. A movie costs $1.20. One of my friends spent ten dollars just going to town, eating a meal, and taking in a movie. On the base, a movie costs only 25 cents, so I only went there. A stamp for mailing a letter cost only 3 cents, but it took 8 or 9 days to reach my mother in Jacksonville. Sending it by airmail took only 2 ½ to 4 days. I had ordered one of the New Revised Standard Version Bibles from the Baptist Book Store before I left Jacksonville. I asked my mother to check on it and mail it to me when they get it. I planned to read that entire version of the Bible while in Alaska, especially since it replaced many of the outdated wording in the King James version.

At the 7th Weather Group Headquarters at Elmendorf, we spent a week being refreshed on our previous weather training. We plotted and analyzed three large maps with weather reports that stretched from China to Europe via the Pacific, United States, and the Atlantic Ocean. We continued for about three weeks, with weekends off. The first weekend I visited the First Baptist Church in Anchorage. I loved that church, especially when one of my friends, Mike Ledbetter, sang "His Eye is on the Sparrow" with his beautiful tenor voice.

1952 At the Hobby Shop at Elemendorf AFB
where I developed film and enlarged photos

On the second weekend, I joined the Faith Baptist Church on the outskirts of Anchorage. It was a very small church that had no building, but they met in a cellar that was the only part built yet. The pastor was Marvin Lytle, and he didn't have many members to help start up a new church. I could help by playing a few of the hymns that

I had taught myself to play. A few of us airmen gathered at a girl's house after church where the family had made an ice skating pond in the backyard by placing boards around it and flooding it with water. This had been done a month earlier, and it was now solid ice.

For our second week of training, we went to an Arctic Training school. It was much like our basic training at Lackland, but it was much more timely considering the part of the world we were now located. We started getting a little snow nearly every day in mid-November. It was just enough to cover everything with a coat of white. Prior to that, the whiteness was only from frost forming on all the fir trees. Around November 20, the temperature rose to 46 degrees and melted most of the snow, but at night the temperature dipped into the 20's and everything was coated with ice. The days were getting shorter and it started getting dark around 3 o'clock in the afternoon.

For my third week at Elmendorf, I was assigned to guard duty. We got our guns and went to our posts for an hour of practice. Sometimes we wore helmets, canteens, and weapons to keep in shape in case of attack. One night I was issued a nice stuffed parka with long nylon "hairs" protruding forward around the hood to keep the frigid air from freezing my face. The temperature had dropped to around 5 degrees, barely above zero. Two days later, I took a hike in about two feet of snow and took a picture along a creek that was frozen, except for a thin blue streak of water in the middle. On the next day, I had 14 hours of KP duty. The work was not too hard, and I enjoyed eating hot dogs for lunch, and roast beef for dinner. I always loved the ice cream bars for dessert; in fact, so much that I even bought a couple more from a few guys that didn't eat theirs.

The best food we had here in Alaska was fish! I loved the Red Salmon and Trout. The Rainbow Trout was seldom smaller than 10 pounds. They say you don't even need bait to catch them. Just attach a piece of bright colored cloth on a hook, and they'll bite. On the first day of December, the sun went down at 2:35 in the afternoon. It didn't come up until 9:35 the next morning. The sun stays so close to the horizon that it looks like a sunset all day. We only had four more days of schooling and finally, it didn't seem unusual to walk back from school at 4 PM in the dark.

On December 7, 1952, I had just heard that they found the remains of a plane that crashed into a mountain. There were 52 victims found in the remains that fell onto a glacier. I didn't know what the trouble was, but they say that when the weather first turns cold, there seems to be a series of crashes each year.

Jack Hall and I went to the Ski Bowl in the mountains about 8 miles from here. The snow was about two feet deep as we climbed about 200 feet to the top of the hill. The temperature has been about 5 degrees all day.

Sunday after church, I went to the place near the western end of 4th Street where there was a powerful telescope. It was pointed at Mt McKinley, 140 miles to the north. The mountain peak reaching 20,320 feet above sea level made it an outstanding sight as the sun illuminated its snow-covered sides. Afterwards, I went back to Elmendorf to finish signing and addressing Christmas cards. I had already done 72, and only had about 20 more to do. The next day I received the color slides that mother picked up from McDaniels Gift Shop. I promptly wrote a letter to her stating that I was sold on taking color slides. You could see so much detail when projecting the pictures on the wall. I was glad that I had bought the 35 mm camera. From Alaska, it would be easy to get the film developed. After taking a roll of pictures in Alaska, I'd simply place the film in a small cloth bag with an address label that came with the purchase. About ten days after mailing it to Eastman Kodak, the color slides would arrive in the mail.

When it was November here, I found the temperatures were not much different from Oklahoma. With highs between 30 and 40 degrees, I didn't need "long Johns". An overcoat and fatigues over my regular underwear were sufficient, but the dampness would penetrate through at night. The food was good, but the milk was "recombined", made from powdered milk. Pure milk costs 20 cents, a whole quart 80 cents. Prices were higher here than in the lower 48.

CHAPTER 17 - Black Pearl of the Pacific

On December 11, 1952, I received my assignment to Detachment 1 of the 7th Weather Group located on a small island called Shemya, near the end of the Aleutian chain. At the Alaska Air Command Headquarters, Colonel Hughes told me that I was picked for this assignment because I did so well on the tests and that it was such a big and responsible job. Before long I would be signing aircraft clearance forms for flights to Alaska and flights to Tokyo. Also, there would be several commercial airlines stopping there since it is about halfway between Seattle and Tokyo. Finally, he said, "I won't tell you it's nice out there because most of the fellows don't like it, but from the weather point of view, it will be very interesting."

My friend, Jack Hall, got the assignment he wanted. He volunteered to be an aerial weather observer on reconnaissance flights to the North Pole. I was happy with the Shemya assignment because I knew I would have a lot of time for reading and studying.

When my church heard that we were leaving, they held a nice farewell party for us after the Sunday evening service. When I got back to the barracks, I wrote my mother a letter telling about my assignment. I also told her that I still hadn't received the new RSV Bible she had mailed. I was worried that it might have been on that plane that had crashed into the mountain.

The next two days we received nearly ten inches snow which caused the flight to Shemya to be postponed for three days. I was happy because I just received my RSV Bible in the mail and I could get started reading it. In the meanwhile, an airman who had been stationed at Shemya came in the barracks and when he learned that I was going there, he told me about the island. I learned that it was only 2 miles wide and 4 miles long, and there were about 300 mainly military personnel there. The coldest temperature ever recorded there was 18 degrees, and the highest in summer once had reached 65 degrees. Almost half of the Pacific storms pass over this station, and it is noted for its long cloudy and rainy periods.

On Wednesday the weather cleared. When I saw the plane that I was going to fly on, I was amazed at its size! It was a C-124 that was being filled with truckloads of supplies that would be carried to that small island near the end of the Aleutian chain. The plane had two levels, the largest and heaviest stacked in the lower level, and we rode on benches in the upper level. After closing the doors and taxiing to the end of a 10,000 feet long runway, the engines were revved at full speed for almost two minutes. Finally, as the brakes were released, the plane moved slowly forward, and then gradually picked up speed as we rolled down the runway for an incredibly long time. Finally, when the end of the runway appeared, the huge machine lifted off the ground and slowly climbed above the Alaskan landscape. It seemed to take at least 10 to 15 minutes to reach an altitude that would clear most of the surrounding terrain.

After six hours, the plane stopped on Adak Island long enough for us to eat a meal, then took off for Shemya. It took only two more hours for us to reach our destination. After my first look at Shemya, I wrote home that "this place is really different from any place I had ever been". We were taken to our living quarters in an old building that formerly was a hospital in World War II. Inside it was quite nice. It had a snack bar, mess hall, place to watch movies, and a barber shop all in one building. The problem was this was near the northern side of the island, and the weather station was on the southern side.

We were halfway between Tokyo and Anchorage, and the nearest large island was Attu, about 40 miles to the west. The Japanese Northern Army had occupied that island during World War II in 1942. Prior to that, two school teachers, Foster and his wife, Etta Jones, had been selected by the Department of the Interior to move to Attu, teach school and set up a weather station at the westernmost island of the Aleutian chain.

A weather report from that site was essential because most storms that struck Alaska came from that area. The island had a small native population of Aleuts, who were a very gentle and friendly people who didn't like the Japanese. The Japanese soldiers had secretly settled on the opposite side of the island while the battle of Midway was taking place to the south.

One day the enemy soldiers came over the mountain, forced the teachers from their home and interrogated Foster about his radio transmissions. His wife saw him surrounded by the soldiers and then shot in the head. The entire account can be read in "Last Letters from Attu", a book compiled by Etta Jones after she was taken prisoner and survived a Japanese POW camp in Japan throughout the entire war.

It didn't take long for me to recognize the weather pattern on Shemya. On my first day, there was a mixture of rain and snow falling. Finally, it all turned to snow. The strong winds blow most of it across the island into the ocean, but in sheltered places, it grows into drifts several feet deep. I was assigned to working the day shift so I could be familiarized with the procedure of plotting reports from trans-Pacific aircraft.

The plane's navigator would send a report of the clouds and winds affecting their flight every hour. We plotted their position and weather data with grease pencil on a large plexiglass- covered map of the northern Pacific Ocean. This helped us prepare forecasts for other aircraft that would fly into those conditions.

I was also learning about Shemya's weather by reading a local forecast study and by talking with each of the forecasters. Our weather was not truly Arctic because we were only a couple hundred miles farther north than Seattle, Washington. We were only 200 miles from the International Date Line, but our time was only one hour different from Anchorage, even though we are 1,500 miles south-west of them.

I wrote home about our mail. It usually went through Anchorage with our supplies. The planes flew in twice a week. On a few occasions, our mail would go through Minneapolis because Northwest Orient Airlines makes refueling stops at Shemya when flying their Stratocruisers across the Pacific from Japan. I explained that our mail should not be addressed to "Shemya AFB". It should address to APO 729 which is the military designation for our part of Alaska.

At the end of my first week, I noticed that we handled more civilian airplanes than military ones. That's because Canadian Pacific and Northwest frequently stop here on their flights between Seattle and Tokyo. It's not only for refueling but that we can provide them with an updated mid-flight forecast. I really enjoy talking with these airmen from the U.S. and Canada, and most of them are interested in the unique weather on this small island. I love describing the latest weather situation affecting us here, as well as the weather they may expect along their routes. I figured that I would be doing flight briefings like these if I go to work for the U.S. Weather Bureau after I get discharged

One very windy day with winds gusting to 50 mph, I was walking along the road next to the runway when I spotted a Northwest Airlines plane approach for a landing. The turbulence was buffeting the plane every which way as the pilot was aiming the nose towards the runway. Suddenly, there was a brief lull in the winds when he was 400 yards short of the runway and in a couple of seconds, the aircraft plummeted to the loose gravel safety zone at the end of the pavement. When I briefed the pilot about the weather, he told me that on that approach, his navigator was lying on his bunk and suddenly was thrust against the plane's ceiling. He was shaken up but fortunately was not injured. A few days later, the plane from Elmendorf, having been held up by foggy weather, came in so late with its 2,000 pounds of mail that we had to wait until the next day for it to be sorted.

CHAPTER 18 - Shemya – A Place NOT God-forsaken

Living on the island was like a religious experience. Walking southward along the road, I stepped out from our living quarters was inspired by God's creation of this sparkling white snow-covered island bordered by the deep blue Pacific Ocean. When I walked around the building and climbed a few hundred feet higher to the northern peak of the island, I caught a similar breathtaking view of the Bering Sea. Sometimes the main road across the island had to be plowed more than once a day. The road which had piles of snow six to eight feet on each side, so it required a large Snow Blower to blast the snow far enough to keep it falling back into the roadway. If a jeep ran off the road during blizzard conditions, it often could not be found until the snow melted in the spring. The roadbed was constructed of ground rock because the island was mainly covered with spongy tundra. There was a rock grinding operation a quarter mile away that provided gravel to maintain the roads when they were not covered with snow.

Speaking of snow, we lived in the old wind-swept hospital complex not far from the top of the island. The windward or south side of the building was where we had no trouble finding access. It was on the back wind-protected side of the building that snow collected nearly roof high. When I first arrived, I was led to the back of the wing that had formerly been the psycho ward during World War II. My bunk was about 8 feet from the back door. Someone had recently opened the door and snow tumbled from a huge snow bank into the doorway. The snow was so dense that it took more than a week to completely shut the door.

Between working, walking, and looking at the unfamiliar features of this volcanic island, I found time to read the first 35 chapters in my new RSV Bible. I compared it with the King James version and hardly noticed much difference. The building that we lived in was a former hospital during World War II. There was a theater in one section of the building about 100 yards down the corridor from my quarters. Fortunately, it had an organ where I could practice playing hymns. I discovered there was another section of the building that had a chapel, but no services were being held. I decided to place a notice on the bulletin board that I would conduct services on Sunday at 11 AM. I also had the service announced on the radio. Around 25 airmen showed up. I started the service playing a few hymns and leading singing. I then went up to the pulpit, read a short passage of scripture, and gave a brief talk, hardly a sermon. After the service, one of the men said that it was just like "being back home", and that I must be Baptist or Presbyterian.

A month later, I met Chaplain Vance N. Clark, who had come to conduct a service in the chapel. Afterwards, he said that he would be gone the next Sunday and asked if I would handle the service in his absence. The organist, Louis Willand, who came with him stayed, and the next Sunday we played an organ and piano duet. Being self-taught, I could mainly just pick out the melody. While I stayed at Shemya, there were many Sundays when both the Chaplain and the organist were gone. On those days, I managed to play the organ, direct the singing, and deliver a message after reading from the scriptures.

I had now read my RSV Bible through Exodus Chapter 13. I thought it was a lot easier to read than the King James version. We had just had a good meal for Christmas. We had roast beef. The vegetables weren't so good, but I liked the peas, the rye bread, and ice cream. The next day, I received 16 letters and two packages. One package was candy from a girl in Stillwater and the other was candy, cookies and a cake from home. I took the cake to the weather station and all the guys were crazy about it. Some of the men weren't there for the cake, but when they came I gave them a box of chocolate covered cherries that I had set outside to cool. They said they really tasted good.

I played bingo the next evening, and guess what I won? A box of chocolates! Afterwards, I walked back to the barracks under a bright full moon. It was shining on a fresh clean snow and on a few white clouds. The mountain peaks eight miles away could easily be seen. That night the temperature dropped to 21 degrees, only 3 degrees from the coldest Shemya ever had. The winds were light so it felt no colder than usual.

In the daytime, we could see the mountains of Attu, 40 miles away, as clear as Agattu's 8 miles away.

On January 8, we had winds blowing 60 mph from a storm that had come all the way from Japan. Instead of snow, we received the first rain I'd seen since coming to Shemya. Three days later, we finally got a chaplain and I wouldn't have to preach anymore. The following Sunday, we got an organist, and I started teaching a Bible class. I was surprised to hear from one of the class members that Matthew 17:21 was omitted in the RSV Bible. One explanation was the verse was not in the original manuscripts, but was added by scribes later; therefore it was entered into the King James Bible. That evening I had reached the book of Numbers as I continued the daily reading of my new Bible.

One of the men in our quarters had finished his assignment and went back to Elmendorf for reassignment. I was fortunate to move into the small room he had vacated. It was only about 8 feet wide and 10 ft deep. It was only furnished with a cot and a desk with a small chair. Having formerly been part of a psycho ward, the door was about 4 inches thick with a small 12-inch square window. The window to the outside was above the cot. Upon examination, I discovered I could string a copper wire through the window outside for a radio antenna. This was my connection for radio programs away from Shemya.

One evening, I picked up a broadcast from WFBK in Sacramento, California. The program was sponsored by Stan's Drive Inn. The announcer said to "drive out tonight for one of our double-burgers and super shakes. All I could do lie on my back and just dream of the food. I send in a letter with a request to play "Let it Snow". A week later, he acknowledged it and played the song. I enjoyed the opportunity to listen to stations in Salt Lake City, Del Rio Texas, Tulsa Oklahoma, Los Angeles, Honolulu and AFRS Tokyo. AFRS was the Armed Forces Radio Service.

Between my room and the barracks-type group of cots near the back door, there was a large room that we called the Day Room, even though some of the guys hung out there playing poker until the wee hours of the morning. Being a conservative Southern Baptist, I didn't gamble, cuss, smoke or drink. As far as going out with girls, I was told that on Shemya, there was a girl behind every tree. The only trouble was the fact that on Shemya, there were no trees!

Actually, there were a few women there. They were airline hostesses that stayed in a restricted part of the base where we very seldom saw them.

For entertainment, the Day Room had a stack of recordings on large records. They contained many popular radio programs of the time. We listened to the "Jack Benny Show", Red Skelton, "Can You Top This?", Edgar Bergen and Charlie McCarthy and a musical program called "Fred Waring and His Pennsylvanians". We played the records on the phonograph in a large Juke Box.

There was a small room behind the Day Room that had a Bendix washing machine. About once a week, I would carry my bag of dirty clothes to the front loading washer. After using the washer, I emptied the lint collector at the bottom of the machine. Occasionally, I would discover a coin or two that had gone through the washing cycle. During my time at Shemya, the best collection I found was I found was a very clean quarter. Twenty-five cents in those days would buy five Cokes!

The mail takes days to go out and a day to come into this lonely island, plus the many miles it must be taken to each of the lower 48 states. On January 3, I received twelve letters written around Christmas that were chasing me through Elmendorf. Some of the guys are scared by rumors that Shemya is just a large rock sitting on top of an underwater mountain peak. It didn't help calm their fears on January 4 when we felt a brief earthquake. I guess you can call it a tremor because it caused no damage and only lasted about 5 seconds.

Chaplain Clarke had temporary duty elsewhere for the first two Sundays in February, so I conducted the morning services those days. I was now reading my RSV Bible in the book of First Samuel, and I found it was a lot easier to understand than the King James. I was surprised to learn the book of Ruth was so short, only 4 chapters within 5 pages. The organist for the chapel returned this month and I joined him in a piano-organ duet, with me mainly picking out the melodies. I always wished I was able to take more than one piano lesson when I was growing up.

We had many sunny days with temperatures between 25 and 35 degrees. I enjoyed the snow showers that we had. They didn't get us wet like the Florida ones did. Most of them were in the form of snow pellets rather than snowflakes. One day, the chaplain, organist and I were walking along the beach and we found pieces of coke bottles that were broken so long ago, that they were worn smooth by the waves, rocks and volcanic soil. I wish I had kept a sample of that soil. The grains were dark gray, smooth and spherical, about 1/8 inch diameter.

My work schedule was 12 hours on and 12 hours off for 4 days, then I got two days off. Time was going fast, and I didn't get tired because I loved the work analyzing maps, reading weather reports and briefing flight crews.

One morning I thought I was going to work at 8, but didn't wake up until 20 minutes after. When I called the weather station to inform them, I found out that I was scheduled off for that day. That was a pleasant surprise!

Since we had received about 80 inches of snow since November, I decided to see if I could build an igloo. After all, this is Alaska and Eskimos live in igloos. I inspected the snow and discovered there was a lot of frozen moisture in the snow. I found that I could cut it into large blocks with a butcher knife. Ultimately, I built the igloo a little over waist high. I paused for a while to take a photo of it, and I'm glad I did because 40 years afterward, I got an e-mail from a friend, Don Grosenbach, who wanted to ask me a question. He said he had a dream that I built an igloo at Shemya, but he didn't know if it was just a dream, or did I really make one? He was happy to learn that it was real, and not just a fantasy.

We didn't get newspapers at Shemya and it was hard to keep up with the news, so I bought a subscription to Time magazine. I had just learned that the Russian leader, Joseph Stalin, had died and I hoped the world situation would become more peaceful. We had some MATS (Military Air Transport Service) planes that were returning some troops home from Korea. Upon seeing Shemya, many of the guys told me that they would rather spend a year in Korea than be assigned to a place like this.

On March 20, I learned that we got a new base commander. They said he is very tough, and he wants to get the base all fixed up. He even wanted to place loudspeakers on top of the building to play bugle calls for reveille, mess (meals), and retreat (sunset). I told my buddies, "Welcome back to the real world!"

Around the first day of spring, we had a lot of nice sunny days, and even though the temperature was near 30 degrees, the wind was light and I felt comfortable outside without a shirt on. A few days later, a Pacific storm blew in with blizzard conditions.

When I got off duty, I got in the Air Force Chevy pickup truck and tried to drive away from the operations building. I could barely see through all the snow and had to stop every ten feet to find the place to turn away from the runway.
The third time I stopped, the front wheels of the truck had gone off the runway, resting on the edge of a 12 feet deep drainage ditch.

When driving this Chevy pickup away from the weather office in a blinding blizzard, I stopped abruptly as the front wheel started to drop into a 12 ft. drainage ditch. Being before the use of seat belts, I was lucky to stop!

Afterwards, I learned that there was no damage to the truck, and our detachment commander congratulated me for being so cautious in driving the truck. I thought I'd be in trouble for having the truck partially extended over the ditch, but instead, Major Wilson congratulated me for driving so cautiously, and when they towed the Chevy back onto the pavement, there was no damage to the truck.

CHAPTER 19 - Close to Nature and a Wider World

With all the water around Shemya, I never had a chance to fish. One day airmen Ahlmark and Dick Paul went down to the Pacific docks to try their luck at fishing. They came back in a couple hours with a big fish story, and about thirty fish to prove it. They said all they had to do was drop their lines into the water and the fish did the rest. Among the catch were some very colorful Japanese perch.

On March 23, the tower had called me for a weather forecast for up to 600 miles west of Shemya. I thought this was strange because our airplanes normally don't fly there. That evening, I learned that one of our weather recon planes had landed at Shemya after being fired upon by the Russians. They had actually flown only 25 miles from a Russian airbase and were very fortunate that they weren't shot down.

Since I had less than a year left on my Air Force enlistment, I inquired the Weather Bureau about working for them. They informed me that upon passing a test that I would be eligible for a $2,950 - $3,410 job as a Meteorological Aid. The also told me that I could become a professional meteorologist by getting a degree from a school like Florida State University. By going into research, I could earn $12,000 a year.

I was still finding many things to fill my time at Shemya. I got a hot plate for cooking in my room. I placed it on my desk and made fudge, and warmed canned food that I bought at the Commissary. I got a book from the library, "Kon Tiki" by Thor Hyerdahl, that was about a raft that drifted with the wind and ocean currents from Peru across the Pacific Ocean to the Polynesian Islands. Reading it, I could relate quite well because Shemya is a small island surrounded by water on all sides. I also continued reading my RSV Bible, now reaching Psalms, the halfway mark in the Bible. This was on May 12 when I felt our second tremor from an earthquake.

On May 28, I stayed up past midnight listening to some operettas. I finally went to bed a little after 4 AM when the siren suddenly sounded an alert. We all went out in the 40 mph wind which was gusting as high as 60 mph, combined with rain and snow. We rushed down to discover the Commissary being consumed by flames, smothered in smoke, and with canned goods exploding skyward like rockets.

The first week of June brought warmer temperatures, but as the moist air from the south passed over our chilly Alaskan waters, the moisture condensed into fog and a dark low overcast. Visibilities were frequently down to 1/16 mile; consequently, planes couldn't land to deliver mail or pick it up. I walked by the mail room and saw tall stacks of letters waiting for delivery. Most of the snow had melted and the grassy tundra was turning green. By June 28, the sun had only been out 8 hours since the beginning of the month.

Finally, the sun broke through and we saw a beautiful blue sky, but there were streaks of steam rising from the wet landscape. I found a place under the northern cliff that was sheltered from the light breeze. Although the temperature was in the upper 40s, the intense sunlight made it feel like it was near 70. When I went back to the barracks, I was red like a lobster. A couple of days later, my skin peeled and many of the guys who had worked outside were all red-faced.

On July 2, this island that had been cloaked in fog for nearly a month suddenly burst forth in beautiful colors. There were mainly purple flowers and yellow flowers that decorated the deep green tundra, a sight that could almost match Alaska's rival, Hawaii. I loved to walk close to the Bering Sea shore and watch the large waves crash against the rocky shoreline. Once I spotted a seal resting on a boulder. He looked like a dog with a fishtail!

On the evening of July 2, we had a very good U.S.O. (United Service Organization) show performance by a man who played the guitar and harmonica at the same time. We cheered him back for about ten songs. Usually, I don't like the shows too much because of their raw jokes, but this was the best one I had seen yet.

One of the airmen never cussed or drank before he came to Shemya, but while here he had a tendency to take up bad habits from anyone he associated with. After a while, he was reassigned, we corresponded with each other. He wrote that he was surprised that I took a liking to him while he was here. As a result, he told me that his knowing me got him to stop drinking and start going to church every Sunday. I had never talked to him that much, but he just watched me and noticed the things I did and didn't do.

On August 2, I was still reading my RSV Bible and had reached the book of Acts. It was about the Jewish conspiracy against Paul and his trip to Rome. I received a letter from Louis A. Willand, Senior Welfare Specialist with the Office of the Protestant Chaplain, commending me for willingly and voluntarily holding worship services at Shemya when no Chaplain was available. I also got a letter from Jack Hall telling me that his wife, Rose, had joined him in Fairbanks. They had a car and a dog. He said his recon plane flew over Shemya every other week, but never landed here.

I was quite stiff and sore from working on our Jeep. They were going to junk it because of a broken hub on the rear axle, but I went to the junkyard and took one off an old Jeep, and put it on ours. I hated to see anything go to waste when it could be repaired and reused.

On August 3, Secretary of State John Foster Dulles' plane landed here because of engine trouble. Fortunately, it was repaired before they were flying the 1,500-mile flight farther over Pacific waters before reaching Japan and Korea. He was going to meet with Korean President Syngman Rhee.

On August 10, I flew on a familiarization route aboard an RCAF (Royal Canadian Air Force) DC-4 airplane. The flight lasted nine and a half hours. In Tokyo, I got on a Rickshaw, which was a two-wheeled cart pulled by a man. He asked if I wanted to be taken to Geisha girl, which is a prostitute. I told him no, then asked him to take me to a park where I could go swimming. We rode past Hirohito's Palace which was surrounded by a moat with weeping willows on its banks. I got to swim in a beautiful large swimming pool that had very tall diving towers at one end.

A few days later it was time to fly back to Shemya. From the airport, I could get a good view of Mount Fuji, which is a 12,000 ft. high volcanic mountain about 80 miles southwest of Tokyo. I had left a roll of film in the desk drawer at the airport, and when I returned I discovered it had been stolen. At least, I still had my camera with film in it to take pictures.

On September 1, I had my 22nd birthday. I didn't have to work that day. I enjoyed sleeping late, cleaning my room, and just relaxing and reading. Shemya gets its mildest weather this month with daytime temperatures near 50 degrees, and I enjoyed spending time along the Bering seashore. One day, I rented a bicycle and rode about 4 miles around this two by four-mile island. There's not as much fog, and it is still another month before we get our first snow. But sometimes, we get very high winds when the typhoons that are far to the south swing far enough north to affect us. One day, our radiosonde airman, Glenn Law, was trying to launch a balloon when a strong blast of wind dragged him several feet before he could release it properly.

On October 13, we got our first snow of the fall, but it didn't stay on the ground. We had been noticing the distant mountains on Attu becoming covered with more snow over the past few weeks. We were expecting a big storm to hit us the next day with winds as high as 90 mph, so I spent the day nailing strips of wood over the tar paper covering the chapel so it wouldn't be torn off by the wind.

A couple of days later, I went to see a movie, "The Clown", starring Red Skelton. He died at the end of the movie which made it very sad. We also saw a short subject about water skiing in Cypress Gardens, Florida. It really looked good to see the warm sunshine again. I went to the dry cleaners to pick up a pair of my light gray, wool pants. I had spilled coffee on them and it didn't come out. I finally decided to rinse them in some warm water and Tide detergent. It turned the water very dark, but the pants came out clean as a whistle!

Things have been changing on Shemya since last summer. The first big change was the removal of the large 35 mm movie projectors, and replacing them with 16 mm ones. The movies still looked good, but it saved a lot of money spent on film. In September, three hundred engineers were shipped out, and there were very few coming in to replace them. They had finally removed the organ from the chapel, and I had just started training my replacement at the weather station. Our commanding officer finally cleared me from duty and gave me a character rating of excellent, and an efficiency rating of excellent.

CHAPTER 20 - Farewell to Alaska

On November 2, our winds started to increase. By evening they reached 70 mph, and the rain was very heavy. I was down to the last two chapters of Revelation in my RSV Bible. I read the next to the last chapter the next morning and the final chapter on the plane flying back to Anchorage. When I got off the plane at Elmendorf, the temperature was only a couple of degrees above zero. They had just turned the water hose on the tennis courts to freeze into a skating rink.

My leaving Anchorage was delayed several weeks, so I had a chance to visit my friends at Faith Baptist Church. I had a very nice dinner that included moose. It was the first time I had eaten any, and it was very tasty. It was a nice reminder of Alaska for me. I finally flew out of Alaska at the end of November and landed at Parks Air Force Base, which was 28 miles east of Oakland, California.

I had to wait there for over two weeks to be processed for discharge because of the large number of airmen being released from duty. I was being discharged from the Air Force three months early because servicemen with less than six months on their enlistment would not be assigned to a new base. I finally received my Honorable Discharge on December 16, 1953.

I bought Greyhound bus ticket for Jacksonville and spent the next 7 days across parts of 8 states. There were frequent stops for meals and for changing passengers. At least, I didn't have to hitchhike, and I learned to sleep while leaning back in the bus seats

CHAPTER 21 - Back to Civilian Life

As a U.S. military veteran, I easily made the transition back to the civilian world. In fact, I was much better prepared than I was from growing up with my family and graduating from high school. The government informed me of my veteran rights and benefits, such as the GI Bill, and most importantly how to obtain civilian employment. The State of Florida Employment Office on Bay Street in Jacksonville made my education and military training available to prospective employers.

I lived with my mother, now a widow, in an apartment on Dellwood Avenue in Riverside. The house was owned by Sam and Louise Mathews. Mr. Mathews was a retired railroad man who greatly assisted mother when I wasn't around. She worked as a cashier at the Arcade Theater on West Forsyth Street.

Working in the box office which faced the sidewalk, she became acquainted with many pedestrians. She enjoyed the work because she always loved people. The salary very low and I wasn't sure that it was a good long-term occupation.

She had attended Trenton Normal School in New Jersey after high school, so I encouraged her to go back to teaching school. Being a primary school teacher, she really helped me and my brother, Richard, get a good basic education in grammar and child development.

Because of my scientific background, I was quickly hired by the Glidden Company on Jacksonville's north side as a Chemical Laboratory Assistant. The company processed pine tree products, called Naval Stores, into turpentine that was distilled to produce useful substances like perfumes and cleaning products.

I became acquainted with fractionating raw liquids to certain temperatures to remove particular substances. The results were used by their chemists to produce a variety of scents, such as lemon, peppermint, and spearmint being a few that I remember. We analyzed the substances through an electro-spectrometer, which identified certain chemicals by their wavelengths. This reminded me of the sun's energy that contained the different wavelengths of X-ray, ultraviolet, visible, and infrared rays.

I worked at the Lab from 4 PM to midnight after attending classes at Jacksonville Junior College (JJC) (now Jacksonville University) in Arlington.

After USAF discharge, George enrolls at Jacksonville Junior College

I started as a freshman, even though I had received 33 semester hours from the Air Force Intermediate Meteorological School at Oklahoma A&M (now Oklahoma State).

The transcript from A&M only showed a 3-semester hour credit for Synoptic Meteorology which I took separate from the USAF School.

The JJC counselor didn't inform me of this during my interview. It was not until I entered FSU in 1955 did I learn that I hadn't received a record of all my semester hours.

I breezed through my College Algebra at JJC because I had already gone through Calculus in the Air Force. My favorite subject was Social Science which I studied under Professor Joseph A. Hauber who enthusiastically helped me connect with the history of my German grandparents. He attended Union Theological Seminary in New York and was fluent in five different languages. He not only taught us Social Science but most importantly the Etymology of words. Since most words have a root from Latin, I then could understand a lot of things I read without actually knowing a new word's definition. Fortunately, I took one year of Latin in high school and two years of Spanish. Another of my favorite subjects was Philosophy which was taught by the acclaimed philosopher and theologian, Dr. James A. Stewart. His teaching of reasoning and logic helped me understand how people could reach different conclusions from the same facts.

CHAPTER 22 - Meeting the Love of My Life

One Sunday, I visited the Riverside Park Baptist Church which was a few blocks from our house. One of the first persons I met was Bob Carter. Bob introduced me to his sister, Virginia. I liked her from the beginning and we began sitting together in church. We soon became Sunday School teachers. Many people said that we looked like brother and sister when together. Virginia impressed me with the confidence of her convictions, and I got the impression that she was very compassionate about other people. In fact, I felt like she would have liked to become a missionary, although I never told her that.

After dating Virginia for six months, I asked her to marry me. We picked out her rings from the Ferrell Jewelry Store at the corner of Main and Monroe Streets in downtown Jacksonville. Virginia had worked at the soda fountain of the Lane Drug Store. I always enjoyed watching a "soda jerk", (not Virginia), making Ice Cream Sodas. I remember the Scarlet Nectar, a four-dip vanilla ice cream soda that was built on a base of red cherry syrup. Virginia also worked for a short time at the snack bar in the Jacksonville Train Terminal at Lee and Bay Streets. When I met her, she had a sales job at Grayson's, a women's apparel store on Laura St. We like to meet for lunch at the lunch counter in the Kress Five and Ten Cent Store on the corner of Main and Adams Streets. We each often ordered one of their delicious hot dogs.

1954 Riverside Park Baptist Church

Virginia's father, Henry Carter, was a carpenter who built houses in Cedar Hills for Charles Scheurer.at the time the city was expanding to the southwest and worked on houses in Alderman Park off the Arlington Expressway during the boom of the late 1950's. His wife, Eunice, was a homemaker and was devoted to working with babies and toddlers in her west Jacksonville church.

A year later, we were married by Reverend Hubert Taylor on June 25, 1955, in the Riverside Park Baptist Church on Roselle Street. Her bridesmaid was Lois Carter, her brother's wife. My best man was my brother, Richard. We spent the night in a motel on Third Street in Jacksonville Beach. There was a dance hall a couple of blocks away that played loud dance music until the wee hours of the morning.

My part-time job after JJC classes at Glidden Chemical Lab with 1948 Ford.

I finally bought my first car, a 1948 four-door Ford sedan. After a month or two, I decided it was too big. I liked the Henry J, a compact car that would be more economical by getting greater gas mileage.

I taught Virginia to drive the car and she shortly got her driver's license with it. She even learned to drive that car with a clutch and stick shift on the hills of Tallahassee. I'm proud to say after more than forty years of driving, she has never had an accident, nor even received a traffic ticket.

CHAPTER 23 - Married Life in Tallahassee

A few days later, we packed our earthly possessions onto a trailer hitched to my car, and drove to Tallahassee where I entered Florida State University where I would be tutored by Dr. Werner Baum who had launched the School of Meteorology just six years earlier and Dr. Noel LaSeur who put me to work compiling Florida's rainfall totals on a comptometer.

The only money I would have would be $125 a month from the GI Bill; consequently, my bride took a job at Sears Roebuck in downtown Tallahassee. She quit that job a month or two later to take a position of cashier at Tallahassee Memorial Hospital. I think God had a hand in that because she turned into an angel who guided my health care many later years that included prostate cancer and two heart attacks.

We moved into an apartment on East College Street that we soon learned had mice. I would set a mouse trap under the sink in the kitchen each evening, and then we would hear the trap snap shut in the middle of the night, or I would look under the cabinet in the morning and find a dead mouse in it. Tallahassee had just started a television station, WCTV Channel 6, about that time.

I wanted to watch more than one channel, so I bought a TV antenna and mounted it on top of the two-story apartment house. I almost had a tragic accident on the roof. It was covered with slate tile and when I straddled the chimney to attach the antenna, my right foot slipped on some moldy slates. If I had put all of my weight on that foot, I would have slid down the roof and dropped about fifteen feet to a concrete pavement. I finally pointed the antenna towards the east and we could occasionally receive a snowy picture of Channel 4's Bill Grove and the 6:30 PM news in Jacksonville. We could also catch the Dothan, Alabama channel on the back side of the antenna.

Before the fall session started at FSU, I got a job with a construction company that installed power poles in Monticello, about 30 miles east of Tallahassee. This was in the day when the holes were dug by hand-operated post hole diggers. Some of the tastiest lunches I ever ate were in the restaurant in downtown Monticello across from the courthouse.

A few months later, we met a lady, Maude Britt, at the First Baptist Church who had a vacant apartment in her new duplex on Park Avenue, just a half block from the FSU Campus. This time I didn't have to climb on the roof for a TV antenna. I bought two 12 feet sections of pipe, topped with an electric motor that could rotate the antenna. With this arrangement, I occasionally received television programs from distant places like Cuba, Texas, and even Buffalo, NY. This was only under unusual atmospheric conditions in the winter when it was cloudy or foggy.

When my college courses began, I tried to supplement our income with such things as selling Wearever aluminum cookware. I was unsuccessful at that, so I finally got a newspaper delivery route for the Florida Times-Union. It was for the "Star-edition", which only went to the black neighborhoods. The only trouble was not many prescriptions were prepaid. For those unpaid subscriptions, I had to go to each house to collect. Needless to say, I barely collected enough to pay for gas and wear and tear on my car.

While working there, we learned of the bus boycott in Montgomery, Alabama after Rosa Parks refused to sit in the back of the bus, which was required under the laws of a segregated south. There was great resistance to desegregation of public school. I frequently remarked to my coworkers in the Times-Union office that I couldn't understand why it was customary to have black maids in white homes raising their children when they didn't want black children integrated with white children in the schools.

I was able to quit delivering newspapers when I got a job working for Dr. Noel LaSeur in the Meteorology Department on Jefferson Street. The department was located in a two-story wooden building on Jefferson Street two blocks from Westcott auditorium. On the second floor, I could read the latest synoptic weather observations on a teletype printer, and see the weather charts on a facsimile machine. There was one room with a table containing electric comptometers where we tallied rainfall totals for more than a hundred recording sites around the state. The calculating machine had eight columns, each containing ten numbers, 0 to 9, with which to tabulate daily totals. I was impressed with the great variations of rainfall around the state.

CHAPTER 24 - Tallahassee and Jacksonville Connections

After the winter term, we began driving to Jacksonville where we stayed at my in-law's house. Our Jacksonville church paid me $25 to clean the buildings on Saturday. On Sundays, I would play the piano if a real pianist was not available. In the summer of 1956, I went to a dentist in Tallahassee for a cyst on the roof of my mouth. He referred me to a dental surgeon, Dr. Fred Mann, who discovered the cyst was caused by an abscess from an infected tooth. Testing the tooth with an electric current proved the tooth to be dead. The tooth was probably injured when I tumbled off my bicycle in 1945. I had a root canal placed inside the tooth, and the cyst was removed in the new Baptist Hospital that had just opened a year earlier.

After recuperation at my in-law's house in Jacksonville, I finally rejoined Virginia in Tallahassee. A few months later, Virginia learned she was pregnant. I remember when we went to the County Fair that fall; we observed a chart that displayed the development of a baby month by month in the womb. After spending Christmas at her parent's house, we decided that she should quit her job at Tallahassee Memorial and live with them until the baby came in May. Fortunately, I didn't have to drive to and from Jacksonville each weekend. My classmate, Windell Dixon, visited his parent's house a few blocks away each weekend. I would ride with him to Jacksonville on Friday afternoons, and ride back to Tallahassee early Monday morning in time for our 9 AM class. This was before Interstate 10. We traveled on the old US 90 two-lane road. There were frequently patches of dense fog in the dips between the hills on the road. It was a beneficial learning experience for us observe firsthand the way fog developed.

During my senior year at Florida State, I spotted an advertisement on the bulletin board on the first floor of the Meteorology building (which was a two-story house that the university had bought). It advertised jobs for meteorologists at WTVT Channel 13 in Tampa. At the time I had no interest in one at a TV station. I preferred the weather station type workplace which was similar to my experience in the Air Force.

Virginia, four months pregnant with our first child, left her job at Tallahassee Memorial hospital to live with her parents in Jacksonville. I stayed in Tallahassee for my last semester exchanging our two bedroom apartment for a single room in a house on St. Augustine Street. A close classmate let me use his kitchen to warm things like soup and canned dinners since the money from the GI bill didn't leave enough to eat in restaurants more than once a day, even though a meal in those days cost only 50 cents.

Our baby was due on May 18, and the FSU Commencement Ceremony was to be held on June 1. Unfortunately, our first son, George Franklin, did not arrive until May 29. In those days, the mother and baby would still be in the Jacksonville's Baptist Hospital until June 2; consequently, I had to receive my diploma without her being present. On June 1, I rode to Tallahassee with her brother, Henry Laverne Carter, and his wife, Janet, to attend the Ceremony. Afterwards, we stopped at an Italian restaurant on US 90 east of Tallahassee for a delicious Spaghetti dinner.

CHAPTER 25 - Brief Weather Bureau Career

Three months prior to graduation, I had mailed my application to the U.S. Weather Bureau. I waited three weeks while living with my in-laws in the quiet neighborhood of Murray Hill in Jacksonville. Finally, one day the doorbell rang. When I opened the door, Roger Plaster introduced himself, informing me that he was Meteorologist-in-Charge, of the Jacksonville Weather Bureau office at Imeson airport. Roger was to become instrumental in directing my training in observation and recording of weather data, aviation forecasting, pilot briefing, and the technique of releasing a weather balloon to monitor wind, temperature, and humidity as it traveled aloft. His efforts on my behalf were supplemented by many others including World War II veterans Bill Hillig and Ken Dieter, technical expert, Harold Quattlebaum, who taught me to use a weather recorder called the triple-register, and Bob Shearston who could dramatically describe his many hurricane experiences on Swan Island in the Caribbean. Over the years I also benefited from networking with notable broadcast meteorologists and hurricane forecasters, Neil Frank and Bryan Norcross.

Many opportunities opened up for me in the Weather Bureau. I quickly advanced from Observer and Public Service forecaster to Aviation forecaster, and finally Quality Control Officer for a new program that trained Federal Aviation Agency (FAA) employees. It was my responsibility to administer tests to certify Flight Service Station employees that would provide weather briefings at various airports over eastern Georgia and South Carolina. I declined an offer to become a computer programmer at the Weather Bureau Headquarters in Washington. I was more interested in Florida and tropical weather.

I realized that a broadcasting career would involve a lot more than just forecasting the weather; subsequently, I searched for a book that would help me in public relations. I found such a book written by Elmer Wheeler called "How to Put Yourself Across". Wheeler was described as America's most successful salesman. As a Christian, I studied the Bible about God's commandments and Solomon's proverbs. After reading the book, I was impressed how much his tips reinforced much of what I had been studying over the years. I had been looking for clues about successful living from biographies of historical people like Benjamin Franklin, Wilbur and Orville Wright and Thomas Edison. Finally, I gave the book to my pastor, Rev. Carlton Owens of the Riverview Baptist Church in Jacksonville.

I was first assigned as Weather Observer at the airport that was originally called Jacksonville Municipal Airport. For the airport's inauguration ceremony in October 1927, Charles Lindbergh arrived with his "Spirit of St. Louis" airplane. It had just completed the first solo transatlantic flight a few months earlier. Here I was 30 years later taking weather observations for airlines like Eastern, National, and United airlines to land and take off. Being near the Atlantic Ocean and the St. Johns River, it was important to report the dangerous fogs that occasionally covered the runways. On one foggy morning in 1957, an Eastern Air Lines Constellation clipped a few tall pine trees short of the runway, crashed and burned killing 12 passengers and 5 crewmembers. Also, the aircraft was transporting the body of a deceased airline employee northward in the casket.

I was excited about my new career. I took weather observations, released radiosonde balloons, and plotted their ascending tracks on a circular plotting board that enabled me to measure the direction and speed of winds aloft at various altitudes. As a weather observer, I had always wanted to see a tornado. Whenever I heard thunder or saw a darkened sky, I would go to an observation deck or up the stairway to the roof to get a better view. I had only been working there nine days while looking at a black sky from the north observation deck when one of my colleagues ran towards me asking, "Where is it, where is it?"

When I inquired what he was talking about, he replied, "The tornado!" To get a complete view of the sky, I ran up the stairway to the roof and only got to see a white tornado about 2 miles to the southwest receding back into the base of a large cloud.

It was a waterspout that had formed over Trout River, quickly retreating skyward after removing some clothes from a clothesline in the backyard of a waterfront home in the Lake Forest section of Jacksonville.

Since weather observations are taken 24/7, my job consisted of working different shifts. It was hard to adjust my sleeping to a regular routine since we worked the day shift only 2 weeks, the evening shift, two weeks and the midnight (until 8 AM) two weeks. In addition, I was always subject to being called in for severe weather, or to replace another employee. But when we enjoy the job we are doing, we don't spend much time watching the clock!

Most of our forecasters were WWII veterans who learned meteorology with the Army Air Corps. One forecaster, John Watson, was temporarily assigned to Eniwetok Island in the Pacific for the atomic bomb tests. We had 12-inch square sticky dust collectors on the roof for radioactivity measurements. We checked these at regular intervals with a Geiger counter.

Here in Jacksonville, we were located below the control tower in the Terminal Building. Adjacent to the weather office was the Federal Aviation Agency (FAA) that directed regional air traffic and transmitted our weather reports to national weather circuits.

The only local radar was located one floor above us in the control tower. Another local radar was at the Jacksonville Naval Air Station about 14 miles south of us. We had a local teletype circuit that we used to send weather reports and forecasts to area radio and television stations and a few public buildings, one of which was the Atlantic National Bank on Forsyth Street.

One of the old-time meteorologists, Harold Quattlebaum, was originally with the downtown Weather Bureau office before it closed in December 1955. He told me about the days when the office printed weather maps and had them delivered by couriers to local businesses and maritime companies. Also, weather reports and forecasts were telegraphed via Western Union to many public outlets. He explained how an ancient recorder, called a triple-register, measured wind velocity each minute, amounts of rain as it fell, as well as the accumulated hours and minutes of sunshine, on a paper-covered drum as it rotated once a week.

CHAPTER 26 - Hurricane Experiences

In 1959, Roger Plaster made arrangements for me to fly with the Hurricane Hunters into Hurricane Gracie in one of their Super Constellations of VW-4 from the Jacksonville Naval Air Station, The hurricane was a category 3 storm about 200 miles east-southeast of St. Augustine, FL. After flying as low as 600 feet at times, the pilot, Lt Cmdr Morgan Divison, flew the plane into a climbing spiral. Upon reaching 10,000 ft. we entered the calm and cloudless eye of the storm.

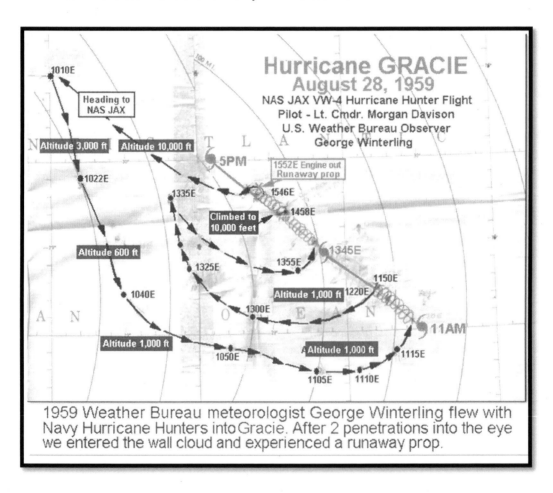

1959 Weather Bureau meteorologist George Winterling flew with Navy Hurricane Hunters into Gracie. After 2 penetrations into the eye we entered the wall cloud and experienced a runaway prop.

From there, the Hurricane Center directed the crew to fly into the northeast eyewall to measure the intensity of the storm's winds. When penetrating the northeast eyewall to measure the storm's intensity, we suddenly experienced a runaway prop. The left engine outside my window began to roar causing the plane to vibrate.

With the danger of a blade flying off, possibly into the cabin, the engine was immediately shut down and we were forced to return to Jacksonville. It was a great disappointment to have such an exciting experience cut short.

On September 10, 1960, all eyes were on Hurricane Donna as it moved into the Florida Keys. As it was turning northward over Everglades City, it seemed to be headed towards northern Florida. Additional personnel were called into the weather office to handle the many inquiries about the storm and what to expect here. As we monitored the storm, we frequently conversed with other broadcast media. Speed Veal was at WJHP. Robert Nichols was the designated meteorologist at the WJAX radio microphone as were the other commentators, Tommy Tucker and Sel Mann.

At the time we couldn't decide if the storm would go to Lake City to our west or right here to Jacksonville. Thirty-six hours later we watched it go east of us into the Atlantic after passing over Flagler Beach to our south.

The highest winds in Jacksonville reached 67 mph, while Jacksonville Beach had 75 mph. Damage in the city was mainly limited to billboards, trees, poles, and wires. Some 100 homes showed minor damage, mostly from roof shingles blown off.

Channel 4 had employed a meteorologist, Frank Forester, prior to this storm. He had come to the weather office several times inquiring about the weather. In addition to being a broadcast meteorologist, he taught a meteorology class at Jacksonville University. It was at this time that I started thinking about taking a similar career path. In those days, most meteorologists worked with the government, the Weather Bureau, and military, or for the airlines.

Colleges taught the science, but very little that would help in television broadcasting. Most TV stations were concerned with appearance and speaking ability. When the weather became life-threatening, looks was not enough. I inquired about positions at two television stations, WJXT Jacksonville and WFLA in Tampa. After doing an audition at each station, I was told: "Don't call us, we'll call you!" It was then that I realized that this was the time to prepare myself for TV.

In the weather office at Imeson, we took turns reporting the live weather reports on radio station WJAX, Jacksonville's Municipal Station. For several years, I had heard

Gerald Davis do these reports. I watched my fellow meteorologist Rex Rhoten's unique way of reporting. He didn't just read the daily weather summary from the teletype. He gave a conversational report by placing the weather map behind the microphone and just talked about the weather. I began doing this, even going so far as sticking a weather map on my bedroom wall to practice my delivery. I even extended this method by verbally describing the weather when driving in my car.

CHAPTER 27 - Buying First Home

My wife, Virginia, and I lived with her parents for 5 months at their two-bedroom home in Murray Hill. It was the gathering place for many family members who lived in Jacksonville and surrounding communities. We drove a few blocks down Post Street to the A&P grocery each week to purchase groceries, went to church together at the Riverside Park Baptist Church where we were married, and enjoyed times at their home with the young nieces that included Barbara Ann and Billie McKee, and Gail and Donna Carter. Virginia's mother prepared real down-home country meals. Whether it was fried chicken or cubed steak, it could not have tasted better. If the pan-steamed okra, the speckled butter beans, rice and gravy along with Ballard's biscuits were not enough, her home-made pecan pie was fit for a king!

Our first home at 3037 Lansdell Drive

Very few homes were air-conditioned, so the day they mounted a Fedder's A/C in the dining room window made summer dining a lot more comfortable. The television was only a few feet away in the adjoining living room. At 5 o'clock in the afternoon, little Gail and Donna were parked in front of the screen as the Mickey Mouse Club came on.

1964 Frankie, Wendy and Stevie
watch Captain Kangaroo on TV

They watched the introduction of M-I-C-K-E-Y-M-O-U-S-E and the roll call of Carol, Bobby, Karen, Annette, and Cubby winding up with Roy and Jimmy the MC's. They would jump up to dance and sing during the program entertaining us grownups more than the TV show. On Saturday nights, we watched Jackie Gleeson and Gunsmoke, while Sunday nights we watched John Daly's What's My Line and Bert Parks' Name That Tune.

We were waiting for our first home to be built off Soutel Drive in Parkview Estates, closer to my work at the airport. Our home had three bedrooms and a large picture window in the living room that gave us a sweeping view of Lansdell and Altamont Drives. The homes were built on the south side of a large sand hill that stretched almost a mile eastward to Lem Turner Road and Henry Kite Elementary School. Our boys, Frankie and Steve would climb to the top of the hill where we could see the skyscrapers in downtown Jacksonville six miles away. The downward sloping road was perfect for coasting in a wagon all the way down to the intersection.

1959 - Frankie riding his "Hot Rod" tricycle

One day, we looked out our picture window and saw our blue and white 1956 Customline Ford car roll backward down our driveway and across Lansdell Drive into our neighbor's driveway. Dashing outside, we saw that Frankie sitting behind the steering wheel. He had pushed the gear shift into neutral, allowing the car to roll away from our house.

Having moved to the northside of Jacksonville, we joined Riverview Baptist Church where Carlton Owens was a pastor. We all participated in Sunday School and the Training Union. The boys were in classes, our new daughter Wendy Gale in the nursery, Virginia taught the Beginners (5-year-olds), and I became Sunday School Superintendent. Herman Mikel was originally the Music Director, but he was followed by Lee Turner. Virginia sang a solo in John W. Peterson's musical Night of Miracles. Lee Turner was a very accomplished pianist who went on to San Jose Baptist Church and made many recordings.

Being a new homeowner, I had to learn how to grow and maintain a lawn. Our house was on the side of a large sandy hill that stretched over a mile from Lem Turner Road to Ridge Blvd. off Soutel Drive on Jacksonville's north side. The builder left mostly sand around the property with small two-inch square grass plugs spaced about one foot apart. The sand had no nutrients, so I frequently picked up a trunk-load of cow manure where we purchased our milk at Pickett's dairy on Old Kings Road.

It was so difficult to grow St. Augustine grass the first two years, that I switched to Bahia grass which would even grow along Florida's roadways with no irrigation or fertilizer. The only trouble was patches of sandspurs that kept mixing with the grass. I finally learned that applying Atrazine in February would keep the spurs from germinating.

I learned that tomatoes and yellow crook-neck squash thrived on spring rains. Our house was on the cold side of the city, so I discovered that tropical things like Rubber plants, Coca Plumosa palms, and Citrus trees needed protection from winter freezes. The only citrus that could survive hard freezes was the Satsuma. The best variety of orange to plant in Jacksonville was the Parson Brown and Hamlin tree because the fruit ripens before the cold winter usually arrives.

In 1960, when Chevrolet came out with the rear-engine compact Corvair, I immediately purchased one from Gordon Thompson Chevrolet on Jacksonville's Southside. The next summer, Virginia, our two boys, Frankie and Steve, and I drove to Houston to visit Virginia's brother in Houston, TX. That was before Interstate 10 was finished so we used two-lane highways - mainly US 90.

On the cold morning of January 12, 1962, I woke up to see our landscape coated with a dazzling coating of ice. Jacksonville had just received 16 hours of freezing rain, only the second ice storm in the city's 120-year history. When I started to go to work, I couldn't unlock my car because of ice in the car's keyhole. I had to pour hot water on it to unlock my car.

While living in Riverview, we had visits from my mother's sister, Hazel Woodfield and her husband, Ed, who lived in Wanamassa, NJ. My grandmother, Mary (Mamie) Cranmer, visited us in Murray Hill when Frankie was born and a second time after Steve was born at my mother's apartment on Dellwood Avenue near Riverside Park. Because of working shifts with the Weather Bureau, I missed spending time with some my visiting relatives, but Virginia filled me in on the family news when I came home.

CHAPTER 28 - Changing Career Path

This chapter calls for a little historical background in Jacksonville broadcasting. In 1949, the television station, WMBR-TV, was added to WMBR, a Tampa 100-watt AM owned by F.J. Reynolds, Inc. that began operations in June of 1927. Reynolds relocated WMBR to Jacksonville in January 1934 and set up offices and studios atop the 13-story Carling Hotel (subsequently known as the Hotel Roosevelt) on West Adams Street. The Washington Post Company sold off WMBR-AM-FM in 1958 but kept the television station, whose call-sign it changed to the current WJXT. In 1951, Windsor Bissell, who had been in radio, became a cameraman and then the producer for WMBR.

When I began my career at WJXT, Windsor was unfailingly patient and knowledgeable as he instructed me on assembling graphics for the weather segments of the news and offering me advice on how to use film, slides, and videotape in addition to my delivery in front of the camera. From his special programs, like "Government by Gaslight," I was impressed how he created a unique reality of the city in the studio. When a background was inserted on a blue, or green, screen in the television called Chroma-Key, we perfected the presentation by pre-taping the segment of a satellite picture and inserting it into the live weather program.

According to Windsor, when Bill Grove was hired by WMBR-TV in the fall of 1952, there was no news department. Any form of news was in broadcast interruptions as bulletins based on Associated Press or International News Service messages on teletype printers. So it was truly a news event when Bill Grove unveiled his news broadcast in the mid-50's called Eye on the News which was sponsored by Cohen Brothers Department Store located in the building that is now Jacksonville's City Hall. And from there, Bill built a solid reputation around responsible journalism and courageous investigative reporting. I could see his early broadcasts while I was studying meteorology in Tallahassee thanks to an antenna I mounted on the roof of my apartment building.

The first TV meteorologist in Jacksonville was Frank Forester. Frank did the 6 PM and 11 PM weather broadcasts at WJXT from 1957 to 1959. After he left WJXT to work with the U.S. Geological Survey in Washington, DC. weather reports were done by news reporters or announcers, as well as a few meteorologists. Even though a few gave satisfactory weather reports, I thought I could serve the station better than any of them.

I wrote a letter to News Director Bill Grove detailing how a qualified meteorologist could provide a much better service to the community and the station's viewers. When I auditioned in 1960, there was no videotape. I had to attempt a weather report in front of management in the studio. I wanted to use the Space-view national weather map I had designed. I needed to find a place that could make a copy of this large 30"x 36" map. I finally found a blueprint company on Bay Street that could make a copy for my tryout.

Afterwards, Bill congratulated me for a having such a visual presentation. And after a few weeks of telling him that I was ready to leave the Weather Bureau and work for WJXT, Channel 4, he offered me the job.

My visual productions continued with the assistance of Production Manager, Pete House, who helped me install weather instruments in the studio. His experience came from working with the Little Theater Group in town. Our Art Department designed the props and sets in the studio. Sometimes they had just stopped painting a new set that was still wet while we were broadcasting.

My first broadcast was on June 11, 1962. Initially, I had to use WJXT's supply of large paper Lambert Conformal projection national maps that we placed on an easel in front of the TV camera. I used a black magic marker to illustrate the weather on a fresh chart for each broadcast. Beginning in September, the news was expanded to 30-minutes and I could use some of my Space-view weather maps that had been printed by Miller Press. After a few weeks of drawing fronts and writing temperatures with a black Magic Marker, I studied the map for a way to improve the report. Since the map was printed on light blue paper to reduce the glare to the TV cameras, the thought came to me that I could paint clouds on it with white Tempera (poster) paint. This would give the clouds a raised appearance over the map. I had seen the first satellite pictures when working with the Weather Bureau, so I gathered the latest weather reports and used my knowledge of weather systems to create the world's first "simulated" national satellite pictures in 1962.

The was just 2 years after the first U.S. weather satellite, TIROS, had been launched, and 4 years before regular satellite images were first distributed by the government. These pictures were only mosaics, a group of smaller adjacent pictures because the first satellites were in low polar orbits. Each picture was only a few states wide, taken as the low polar-orbiting satellite passed from north to south or south to north over a rotating earth. We received these pictures on the newsroom's Wire-photo/fax, issued by the Environmental Science Services Administration (ESSA). By 1970, they had assembled a worldwide mosaic where I could show the disastrous East Pakistan (Bangladesh) cyclone that killed more than 200,000 people. The ultimate, a global view of weather systems were not available until the geostationary satellites were placed in orbits 22,300 miles above the earth in 1974 and 1975.

When I started my television career, news broadcasts were much shorter. The evening newscasts had been only 15 minutes long - five minutes of news with Bill Grove, five minutes of sports with Dick Stratton, and finally my five minutes of weather. This was followed by only 15 minutes of national news - CBS news with Douglas Edwards. In September 1962, the local newscast was expanded to 30 minutes and called Newsnight. That's when Walter Cronkite took over the CBS Evening News.

The biggest news stories in 1962 were related to Cuba's Dictator Fidel Castro turning Cuba into a Communist nation. A failed invasion at the Bay of Pigs by Cuban exiles in August was followed by the buildup of Russian bases in Cuba. When it was learned that there were nuclear-armed missiles there that threaten the United States, President Kennedy warned Russian Premier Nikita Khrushchev that the U.S. would not allow offensive weapons in Cuba. In October, the gravity of the situation was brought home to me when I was stopped by a freight train on Atlantic Blvd. that was southbound loaded with tanks and artillery. That evening, our News Anchor Jim Waldrup attempted to clarify the situation but concluded his report by saying, "I placed a call to the White House, but they still haven't returned my call!"

In November 1963, I was at my desk in the Newsroom when the Associated Press teletype bell started ringing 10 bells. Next, the Bulletin was printed that John F. Kennedy was shot and they were driving him to Parkland Hospital in Dallas. About 15 minutes later it stated that the President was dead!

A few days later, the family was watching the scene in Dallas where handcuffed Lee Harvey Oswald was being taken from the courtroom toward the jail. Suddenly, Jack Ruby, a well-known restaurant owner who frequently visited the building, lunged towards Oswald and fired two or three fatal shots at the suspect.

Starting at a TV station with no prior experience, I had to learn about the time signals given by the Floor Director's hand. His fingers told me the number of minutes left. Crossing the forearms meant only one-half minute longer, and winding the hand meant less than 10 seconds left, and the hand slicing across the throat meant cut or stop. Everything had an allotted time so that commercials, station breaks, and network programs inserted on time. The network was received by coaxial cable. Occasionally, construction or other impedance would interrupt the cable. In this case, the TV screen would display a notice "Trouble on the Cable" or something similar.

I also had to learn about the need for applying facial makeup. For men, it was to hide what was called "5 o'clock shadow", the dirty face look by whiskers on a man's face. Since all of the facial skin had to match in appearance to the camera, I had to apply Max Factor pancake to the entire face, then apply powder to reduce the shine. I always washed it off immediately after the show, but a few of our staff left it on for the late evening show.

Many media personalities are very conversational. Dick Stratton, who did our Sports, often continued talking, even as the Floor Director kept giving the cut signal in front of him. I was the opposite. I was not very comfortable with making small talk. There had to be a purpose in what I was saying.

1962 Starting on Midday at Channel 4

For this reason, the Station Manager, Glen Marshal, assigned me to the Midday program which opened with a panel and conversation. This was easy for me because I could feed off each person's remarks. In fact, on live TV that can be dangerous. But the fact is people's words can reveal too much about a person.

One hot summer day, I placed a thermometer in a car to reveal how hot it got inside. When I told Dick Stratton that it was 110 degrees, he asked me "Where are you going to take the temperature next?" I couldn't think of anything but to just look back at him and say, "You'd be surprised!"

We had a night watchman, Harold Benn, who came to Jacksonville from Connecticut. He enjoyed telling me about his experiences with hurricanes Connie and Diane in 1955 that came with less of a week apart. He had a vivid memory of the disastrous floods that ripped through the river valleys racing towards the sea.

I always wanted to share more than just weather maps with my viewers, so I purchased a surplus World War II 16 mm Victor camera from a pawn shop on Main Street and took pictures whenever I encountered a thunderstorm and flooded streets, the ladies' skirts on a windy day at the Prudential Building, or the boater seeking shelter from the white-capped waves of the St. Johns River.

WJXT News Room 1963
John Thomas Cliff Ransey Bob Atkins
back of Gordon Robbie Bill Grove Bill Blackburn

CHAPTER 29 - Life as a TV Celebrity

When the County Agricultural Fair was in town, Channel 4 had a booth for people to meet our on-air personalities. They also made life-size photos of each of us for the times we couldn't be there. One of them was a cutout of Henry Baron, known as Ranger Hal who had a very popular morning kid's show. When the Fair closed, all of the props were placed behind the Midday set in the studio. One afternoon, Dick Stratton took the cut-out of Ranger Hal and placed it inside the janitor's closet, facing the door. Early the next morning, Wesley Stewart was the first one to come into the building. When he opened the door to get his broom, he nearly jumped out of his skin! Wesley was a very talented artist. He could make all kinds of figures from toothpicks and a bottle of Elmer's glue. He created animals, cars, and trucks, houses, and merry-go-rounds. He frequently won awards at the County Fair.

The employees who worked at Channel 4 from its beginning in 1949 throughout the 50's and into the 60's were very clever in creating illusions on television. Not long after I started at WJXT, I told Dick Stratton that I could make him disappear. Unknown to him, we taped the opening of the Midday Show desk with three of us seated, but his chair vacant. The show started as usual with the four of us seated. Claude Taylor, the newsman, and Phyllis Hanskat, the co-host, sat to Dick's left and I sat to his right. After sharing introductory comments with each other, I stated to Dick that I had talked with a Magician that taught me how to make someone disappear. When he asked how, I pointed at him and said, "Pow!" At that instant, the Director punched up the tape with him missing. He stared at the monitor in disbelief as he saw the three of us still there, but he was gone.

Our business manager, Jerry White, told me about the Jacksonville Power Squadron that met on the former Gibbs Shipyard property at the foot of Hendricks Avenue. They had asked me to attend their regular meeting and teach a Weather Course to area boaters. I also was invited to speak about weather to the Outboard Sport Fishing Club at Mayport's Monty's Marina by Paul Mains. Having been a judge at the Northeast Florida Regional Science Fairs for many years, I was invited to speak to the Live Oak Kiwanis Club by E.K. Hamilton, Lieutenant Governor of Kiwanis. E.K. was from McAlpin which was not far from my wife, Virginia's, birthplace in Pine Mount.

The Channel 4 News Department was intensely focused on Jacksonville politics and Community Affairs. Norm Davis had produced a series of Project 4 programs; one of the first I remembered was of an open-heart surgery operation in the early 1960's. Jacksonville was very progressive in some areas; especially with regard to transportation. We had a system of expressways even before the interstate system reached our area. When it came to weather, it was pretty well left up to me. In fact, I was surprised one day when Bill Grove suggested that I attend an Agricultural Conference in Lakeland, FL where I learned about Frost-Freeze forecasts and citrus protection. It was there I met Warren Johnson, head of the Weather Bureau's forecast office in Lakeland. I remembered using his forecasts while working at Imeson airport and considered his forecasts the most accurate when it came to low temperatures.

I was always interested in local impact weather events, among them being the beach-eroding northeasters along our coast. I was aware of 1932 one that caused one half million dollars damage, and the 1947 one that tore out large sections of seawall. Northeast winds are a seasonal occurrence along our coast, mainly during the fall and winter. But on November 28, 1962, I saw the granddaddy of northeasters coming.

I had a bold headline on my local forecast map that stated. "A Real Northeaster!". That 3-day northeaster tore up much of the boardwalk and seawall at Jacksonville Beach that caused about 2 million dollars along our northeast Florida coast. I had filmed the frantic efforts to save the sea wall as workers were tossing bags of sand over the wall in an attempt to save it. That film was erroneously labeled Dora when the film was replayed a few years later.

On December 5, 1962, our General Manager, Glen Marshall, received a letter from W.W. Stuart, Resident Manager of Hudson Pulp and Paper Corp. of Palatka, FL that expressed his disappointment in Channel 4's weather presentations prior to my employment. He stated that he had lived on the west coast, in New England, in South Carolina and has traveled extensively over the country. He wrote, "In my opinion, the presentation that Mr. Winterling is making is the best one that I have ever seen".

One week after that, the most severe freeze since 1899 hit Florida. Jacksonville's low temperature was 12 degrees which killed many large camphor trees and Australian pines. Orlando had a low of 20, and Tampa went down to 19 degrees. After these events, I was asked to speak many times at civic clubs, churches, and schools. I often spent 30 minutes afterward answering questions about the weather and cycles. A second damaging northeaster hit on February 3-5, 1963, causing one million dollars damage. The property where the boardwalk and seawall once stood was a pile of mass destruction. The battle to stop the devastation from ocean waves included dumping refrigerators, stoves, washing machines and even old car bodies into the churning water.

In 1963, I was elected Chairman of the Northeast Florida Branch of the American Meteorological Society. Vice Chairman was Joe Sassman, who took over my former job in the Weather Bureau as Quality Control Officer for Federal Aviation Agency flight briefers. The NEFBAMS (Northeast Florida American Meteorological Society) were very useful sounding boards for discussing recent weather events.

I also met a group of youngsters at the Children's Museum in Riverside. The following year we met at the new Museum of Science and History (MOSH) near Friendship Fountain. The height of its towering spouts of water was adjusted by a wind anemometer that kept the spray from soaking spectators in the park.

We formed an organization called Jacksonville Weather Watchers. Most of them participated in reading their rain gauges and reporting the daily total to me so I could report neighborhood weather to our TV viewers.

These boys had very successful lives. Bill Riebsame Travis became an author of several environmental books and taught at the University of Colorado in Boulder, and Charles McCool who had served as City Manager of Florida cities that included New Port Richey and Daytona Beach Shores. Don Montague originally became a helicopter pilot, then an airlines pilot and Daryl McCollister became a TV weatherman in Jacksonville and Chattanooga, TN. Jeff Sheffield became director of North Florida Transportation Planning. Channel 12 Meteorologist Bill Zeliff was instrumental in obtaining weather instruments for the Museum, directed by Doris Whitmore.

CHAPTER 30 - Effect of Career on Family

While working with the Weather Bureau at Imeson Airport and living in our first house in Riverview, I often worked nights or evenings; consequently, I had time to spend at home. Some of that time I spent in the yard trying to get the arid sandy property landscaped by hauling sawdust from an old mill in Oceanway. Virginia kept the home spotless while the boys played in the backyard.

We occasionally had visits to the hospital. Our second child always seemed to be the one involved. The first time while only a few months old, Stevie got a smallpox vaccination that had caused an infection in the folds of his neck. He spent a week in Wolfson Children's Hospital. A little more than a year later, he was playing on the swing set and encountered sharp pains in his side. He was diagnosed with a hernia and went to the hospital again for surgery.

After I began working at Channel 4, I worked from 10 AM to Midnight. I mainly had time with the family on my dinner break or on weekends. Now as a public figure, my two sons, Frank and Steve, were in Elementary School and were frequently asked if they were going to be a weatherman like me. Both of them were mainly interested in athletics, playing organized baseball and football. When Frank joined a Tadpole baseball team, the Giants, they went to a playoff his first year. I remember being told of an inning that finished with a triple play. To this day, I have never seen one!

Both boys played baseball with the Sans Souci organization. When their games were moved to Fletcher Morgan Park behind Hogan-Spring Glen School, Virginia and I operated the Concession stand, assisted by Bill and Arie Willis and Roy and Marie Feltman. Our boys were both on their Junior and Senior High School baseball teams.

Frank was an excellent pitcher, but one Christmas he received a Boy Scout pocket knife. Unfortunately while closing it, he cut his index figure. We met a surgeon, Dr. Albert Fechtel, at his office who gave him stitches and he returned to the mound the next spring. While in high school, Frank discovered a lump below his shoulder on his right arm. It was not long after he had watched the TV movie about Chicago Bear Brian Piccolo who lost his battle with cancer. We were very concerned as he was admitted to Memorial Hospital, but much relieved to learn that it was only a blocked duct to a lymph gland.

Frank was a pitcher at Englewood High School and went to Central Florida Community College in Ocala on a scholarship, but his interest turned to criminology. After attending the Police Academy at Jacksonville's FCCJ north campus, he worked with the Jacksonville Beach Police Department. He decided to work for United Parcel Service (UPS), even working overseas one year. He then worked with a landscaper before moving to the Atlanta area to work for a Security company.

Steve grew up to be an assistant coach under Mike Martin at FSU. The Seminoles played in the College World Series in Omaha. Being an optimist, I had purchased airline tickets two months earlier so than Virginia and I could spend a week at this Classic event. After more than 5 years at FSU, Steve became head baseball coach at Pasco-Hernando State College in Port Richey, Florida in 1991. In 2013, he became Athletic Director.

Just nine months after I was hired by Channel 4, our daughter, Wendy Gale, was born. It was a blustery March day when I took Virginia to Baptist Hospital for her delivery. We left the hospital five days later. It was a pleasant spring day when the high temperature was 77 degrees and Wendy weighed 7 pounds, 7 ounces. She was like a doll when we brought her into our home, very calm and seldom crying.

1963 – Welcome to this world, Wendy Gale Winterling!

In the summer of 1964, we rented a cabin at Goldhead State Park near Keystone Heights. The crystal clear blue waters were surrounded by a powdery, soft white sand beach. Wendy, being 16 months old, couldn't walk on the sand; therefore I had to carry her wherever we went. Upon returning home, she never had to be carried again. She walked on her own two feet ever since. Over the years, she accompanied us to her brother's ball games. When she started piano lessons and was performing in recitals, neither of the boys went to watch her play the piano to return the attention she gave them when they were playing ball.

My greatest regret with working at a television station came in 1973 when I had to miss my 10-year old daughter's baptism. That evening, I had two Sunday evening broadcast assignments, one reporting the 6 PM weather, the second being part of a live Sunday evening show called "Sunday Evening with Pat and Jeff". This was not the first family event my hours at Channel 4 made me sacrifice. My wife, Virginia, had to attend several family funerals over the years. In spite of these sacrifices, she was able to appreciate Channel 4's "50 Years of George Winterling" celebration in 2012.

But going back to Wendy's childhood, she took up the flute and played in the school orchestras, and I usually could accompany Virginia to these performances. Her brother, Steve, played the trumpet and triumphantly played "Charge" during the basketball games at Englewood High. Virginia was a busy homemaker, keeping an immaculate house, doing the laundry (without a drier), washing the dishes (without a dishwasher) and providing transportation to school and ball practices.

I had taken a small cut in salary when I left the Weather Bureau to venture into television broadcasting. Neither of us came from families that had resources to help us with our expenses. We had to borrow money from a Loan company for the down payment on our house and we bought the furniture for our home on time. We were always making car payments and refinancing loans from the Finance Company that was charging us 36 percent annual interest. When Visa and Master Charge offered us cards, we could finally reduce our interest payments to 18 percent. Nevertheless, we struggled through our children's school years providing a home and supplying their needs.

CHAPTER 31 - Connecting with Viewers

In 1966, CBS and Channel 4 changed their programming from black and white to color television. WJXT had two large General Electric color cameras in the studio. Since they contained vacuum tubes, they had to be turned on and warmed long enough to synchronize the red-blue-green components so that a Black and white test pattern would be viewed as strictly black and white with the color camera. If color components were not perfectly balanced, the camera would portray the test pattern with a tinge of color on a color TV.

To enhance our on-air appearance, our Station Manager, Jim Lynagh, arranged for those of us who appeared on camera to select color ties and shirts at the Ivey's Department Store in Regency Square. At the time, the style of neckties suddenly went from slim and narrow to as wide as five inches. The bright red, orange, purple and green neckties were worn on top of solid colored dress shirts. People with color TV's were dazzled by the vivid colors, but since color TV's cost near one thousand dollars, most viewers were still watching on black and white sets.

We had several excellent news reporters that I was privileged to know. Bruce Hall, Randall Pinkston, and Steve Kroft advanced to CBS News. Wayne Seal was a promising newscaster who joined WCIV in Charleston, SC but met a tragic death in the crash of an Eastern Air Line plane approaching the Charlotte, NC airport. Mike Patrick started at Channel 4 and went on to become one of the best sports announcers on ESPN. One day Jim Lewis invited me to go a Men's Hair Stylist, B.J. Combs, in the Universal Marion Building adjacent to Ivey's downtown. When I joined WJXT, I changed my hair from a crew cut to a parted slick "Wildroot Crème Oil" one. After B.J. blow-dried and razor cut my hair, it made my head look much better for television, especially the back side when I turned toward the maps while explaining the weather.

While working with the Weather Bureau, I was aware of the concerns of farmers south of Jacksonville in St. Johns County. There were large farms where cabbage and potatoes were grown. Cabbage was usually planted in the fall because the plants can usually withstand the frosts and light freezes of early winter. But potatoes are not planted in the fall because winter freezes would usually destroy the crop. During the winter of 1963-64 one potato farmer, Ed Thigpen, gambled on a mild winter and planted his potatoes in the fall. His plants flourished as temperatures continued mild. In

February, I drove to his potato farm where has was able to harvest a bumper crop when neighboring farmers were just planting. He had the advantage getting a higher price for his crop than the ones that were harvested three months later. I filmed the sorting and packing process to share with our Channel 4 viewers. Thigpen talked with me about agriculture and weather and invited my wife and me to their house where we enjoyed a delicious home-cooked meal.

On one Saturday morning, I learned of tornado-like damage on Jacksonville's Westside A tropical low from the Gulf coast had passed over northeast Florida causing high winds in the Normandy-Park Street section of Jacksonville. Damage exceeded $300,000 as it downed WPDQ radio towers on Normandy Blvd. I surveyed the area and filmed where large oak trees were uprooted near Cassatt Avenue and Park Street since people in most parts of the city were not aware of the local event. On summer afternoons, I frequently drove to film areas where thunderstorms flooded streets, downed trees and produced brief isolated tornadoes. Those were the days before Doppler radar and the Weather Bureau was not aware of those events. These were the days when the newscasts seldom reported isolated local weather variations, but they were a regular part of my weathercasts.

CHAPTER 32 - Significant Weather vs. Major News

On June 6, 1968, Tropical Storm Abby moved across our area on the morning that presidential candidate Robert Kennedy was assassinated. I came to the TV station around 7 AM and CBS had continuous coverage of the event. But torrential rains and fifty-mile per hour winds were approaching our southeast Georgia and northeast Florida viewers. Our television station was their main source of weather information. This was before the Chiron crawl system was developed. The only method we had to run crawl information was to use a typewriter with a white ribbon to print white letters on a two-inch wide black plastic tape. The tape would run in front a small TV camera that inserted it to the bottom of the TV screen. To illustrate the location of the storm, I pasted a tiny white map of our area and attached a black circle (from black art paper from a hole-puncher) to portray the latest storm position. By this method, I conveyed reports of the storm that dumped 6 inches of rain and brought 66 mph winds to the airport and 71 mph winds to Jacksonville Beach.

On August 24-25, a powerful category 4 hurricane, Cleo, ripped across southern Hispaniola and Cuba on a course toward southern Florida. The mountains of Cuba had reduced the hurricane to tropical storm strength and it was expected to pass only a few miles east of Miami on the night of August 26. But the storm rapidly regained hurricane-force strength over shallow waters near Biscayne Bay that were much warmer than the offshore Gulf Stream current. This caused the weaker western side of the hurricane to suddenly approach 100 mph shortly after midnight. When wind gusts reached 135 mph, Miamians who had been told that the hurricane force winds would pass a short distance offshore were rudely awakened by the hurricane's fury.

Afterwards, U.S. Senator George Smathers asked for an investigation of the Miami Weather Bureau. Gordon Dunn, an experienced hurricane forecaster, detailed reasons why there was an unforeseen strengthening of the storm in the Monthly Weather Review's published summary of the 1964 hurricane season.

The key to the danger for Jacksonville was whether the storm would weaken and remain mainly over land between Miami and Jacksonville, or whether it would emerge into the Atlantic around Cape Canaveral and intensify to a strong hurricane off our coast. I stayed on air all night, reporting the storm's center each hour. It was a detailed roadmap that I had pasted on a poster board. From the each of the hourly weather reports from coastal weather stations, I placed a black dot for the storm's center position and shaded the area within 15 miles each side of the dot to represent the storm's threat of strong winds.

The track continued to show the storm moving towards the north-northwest, causing most of the storm to remain well inland. Cleo's rains were cooling the storm more than the peripheral offshore cloud bands could maintain hurricane force winds. The shocker was when I saw that Daytona Beach was reporting a south wind of 55 mph at 5 AM while the Hurricane Center said that the storm had returned to the Atlantic and was east of New Smyrna Beach. This could not be true because winds spin counter-clockwise around the low indicating, the center was still well inland. If Cleo was over the ocean southeast of Daytona, their winds have to come from the north.

I reported that Cleo was still weakening and that it would continue to weaken as it moved through the Jacksonville area around noon. Consequently, our highest wind at Jacksonville Beach was a 50 mph gust, and Jacksonville's Imeson Airport reached only

43 mph. And we were under a Hurricane Warning all that time! The Hurricane Center was probably overly cautious after the surprise strike at Miami the day before.

1964 - On the air for 24 hours tracking Hurricane Cleo

CHAPTER 33 – Dora - Jacksonville's First Full-force Hurricane

My first concern following Cleo was the fact that we were under a hurricane warning for more than 24 hours for winds that were no higher than 50 mph. On Monday, August 31, I described what Jacksonville's greatest hurricane danger would be, one that struck our coast full-force from the Atlantic, not weakened from passing over land. Little did I know that we would face that danger in a little more than a week.

During the first week of September, I watched the next tropical storm form over the mid-Atlantic Ocean well east of the Leeward Islands. It was headed in the direction of Bermuda, so I thought most storms on this course would miss the U.S. mainland. Over the weekend I watched another hurricane, named Ethel, catching up with Dora on nearly the same track. When Dora made a turn towards the west, I knew that Jacksonville and northeast Florida would be faced with a real hurricane threat.

At the time, I was the only weatherman at Channel 4. I began my day around 10 AM and was not finished until 11:35 PM when the late show came on. Taking my 16 mm Victor camera, I filmed all of my hurricane preparations at home. I moved all the kid's toys, the patio furniture, trash cans, and plants inside. I drove stakes in the ground and used rope to brace my younger trees and secure my aluminum patio roof. I filmed my battery radio, including the car radio, and the canned goods among other things necessary during a hurricane. After checking weather reports at the Weather Bureau office, I filmed the low roadway that would be flooded by Trout River at Main Street.

With the films ready for processing in Channel 4's lab, I made my weather report on the Midday Show at 1 PM and prepared the weather office for the long hours I would face for at least three days. In my 6 PM Newsnight report on Monday, September 7, I indicated that Dora would come ashore near St. Augustine. I wrote a large 100 over the St. Johns River south of Jacksonville and circled it, stating that we could expect 100 mph winds from Dora around Wednesday. This was not generally believed because the Weather Bureau advisory was largely focused on Dora relative to the Kennedy Space Center at Cape Canaveral.

I was certain that a slight jog to the northwest would cause Dora to slam the coast near St. Augustine. With no weather stations out in the Atlantic, I was unable to track the exact center of the storm. I studied each the hurricane advisory from the Miami

Hurricane Center and compared it with wind and barometer reports from coastal stations, like St. Simons Island, Mayport and Daytona Beach.

On Tuesday, September 8, Dora continued westward around 15 mph closing in from 480 miles off Cape Canaveral to within 150 miles. The storm's peak winds decreased slightly from 130 mph to 125 mph. I was reporting the latest information on the storm hourly with Channel 4, even staying on the air throughout the night into Wednesday. After broadcasting information about sections of the city that were in danger of serious flooding, our Program Director, Leonard Mosby, walked by my office and said, "Keep it brief!" I thought this was strange since we were about to be hit by the strongest hurricane in the city's history. I presume he was primarily concerned with programming and interference with running commercials.

By 11 AM on September 9, the Weather Bureau acknowledged that Dora was headed towards St. Augustine. Dora was centered 90 miles east-southeast of St. Augustine with 115 mph winds moving northwest 10 mph.

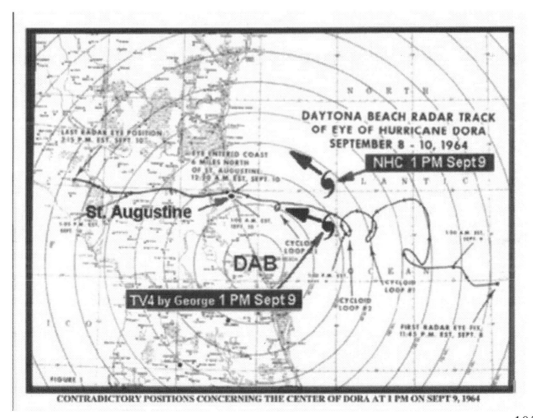

CONTRADICTORY POSITIONS CONCERNING THE CENTER OF DORA AT 1 PM ON SEPT 9, 1964

Suddenly, the next advisory at 1 PM stated that Dora was centered 65 miles east-northeast of St. Augustine. I had been monitoring the Daytona Beach reports and saw that the barometric pressure was still falling from 29.41 inches to 29.23 inches, an indication that Dora was still closing in on the coast east-southeast of St. Augustine. After reporting this discrepancy, I received word from Jacksonville Naval Air Station that my storm position was correct! With the wind and rain squalls increasing over Jacksonville, we suddenly lost power. Having no emergency generator, Channel 4 was off the air, but I continued giving reports on the storm via telephone. Bill Greenwood called me from WMBR radio in Jacksonville, and I was asked by stations as far away as Douglas, GA for storm reports.

Finally, around midnight, Dora's eye came ashore at St. Augustine. The storm surge in the St. Johns River was about 5 feet. The driveway to the station on Southampton Road was covered by two feet of water. Shortly after midnight, I got a call from a woman in Green Cove Springs who said that the winds and rain had stopped and she could hear flocks of birds outside. When phone calls ceased, I drove through the city towards my house, surprised that the winds were not as high as they were earlier in the evening. They were only 30 to 40 mph. Having been awake for 40 hours, I went into my home and quickly dropped off to sleep.

After breakfast on Thursday morning, the sun came out and the northeast winds had subsided and shifted to the southeast. I saw that the trees that I had braced from the storm still stood, so I drove through Riverview to Carbondale Drive and filmed a neighborhood with a dozen snapped pine trees around houses near Trout River. I then drove via Broward Road to Main Street where the swollen river was still flooding part of the roadway. Upon reaching Channel 4, I discovered the power had been restored. After removing the film from my camera for processing, I saw Glen Marshall, our Station Manager. He told me to take the next two days off. Since I was the only meteorologist at the station, I had to continue doing my three regular weather reports, the Midday Show at 1 PM and the 6 and 11 PM newscasts.

Upon driving home, I stopped at the 7-11 in Lake Forest. The man at the counter told me that he had heard that Dora was coming back our way. He was right! Sure enough on Saturday, my day off, the storm had raced eastward across southern Georgia. A backlash band of thunderstorms raced eastward through the Jacksonville area causing us to lose power again, but this time only for a short time.

I was given a lot of credit for giving such an early warning for Jacksonville's first direct strike by a hurricane from the Atlantic. After the storm, Channel 4 published a reprint of an article in the Gainesville Sun by Sam McGarvey that described my correction of Dora's position because of the falling pressures at Daytona. I was amazed and amused that after warning local residents so far in advance of Dora, my name had become a household word in northeast Florida and southeast Georgia!

Fortunately, all of northeast Florida and southeast Georgia was well prepared for the storm, thanks to the combined efforts of people like Roger Plaster, Meteorologist in Charge of the Weather Bureau in Jacksonville, Jack Weatherford, Director of local Civil Defense and Sheriff Dale Carson. Richard Brooke and the American Red Cross coordinated the dozens of storm shelters around Jacksonville, while dozens of public officials along with fire and police departments all over northeast Florida and southeast Georgia are among the thousands of unsung heroes that served our citizens. Dora had caused around 250 million dollars damage. There were no deaths in northeast Florida counties. Elsewhere, there were only 5 fatalities reported, one of which occurred by drowning in the flood from 17 inches of rain that fell in Live Oak.

Hurricane Dora downed large trees to block sreets in many neighborhoods

Hurricane Dora's 10+ storm surge hits Jax Beach.

More than 17 inches of rain flooded downtown Live Oak, FL

CHAPTER 34 - Extreme Weather - Cold

Jacksonville's proximity to the Atlantic Ocean, plus its southerly latitude, causes its winters to be relatively mild. But it is not immune to occasional intrusions of bitter polar or arctic air. During the winter of 1958, January, February, and March were unseasonably cold with the month of February having 13 days with low temperatures below freezing. In those days, many homes were poorly insulated and depended on space heaters to stave off the cold. On February 13, northeast Florida and Jacksonville received 1.5 inches of snow, the first snow to cover the ground in 59 years. This was the year after the Russians launched the first man-made satellite and America was shooting many rockets into space in an attempt to orbit the earth, too. Many people wanted an explanation for such a climate change to colder weather because we had been experiencing a string of mild winters that peaked around 1950. It was thought by many that the rockets were causing changes in the upper atmosphere.

In January 1960, there were six consecutive days below freezing, the most since records began in 1872. In that year, December had ten consecutive days at 32 degrees or lower. It was the coldest December in 25 years. In 1966, an arctic cold outbreak dropped the temperature to a morning low of 20 degrees, followed by an afternoon high of only 33. June in that year was the coolest on record, prompting me to write an article for the April 1967 edition of *WeatherWise Magazine*, "Florida's Recent Cool Cycle Commencing with Snow at Jacksonville."

In 1975, I met Dr. Steve Browder, head of the Physics Department at Jacksonville University. He invited me to teach Meteorology as Adjunct Professor at the university that gave me the opportunity to share the wonders of weather with a younger generation. This was a time before the Weather Channel, and TV weather reports were mainly relegated to only three minutes in the 30 minute evening newscasts. These young people were about to experience some of the coldest weather in Jacksonville's history. The first was the winter of 1976-77, our coldest winter on record. The December-January-February average temperature was 48.9 degrees. The month of January averaged only 44.0 degrees. A persistent southward shift of the polar jet stream caused Palm Beach, FL to experience what was normal for Jacksonville, Jacksonville's January was normal for Birmingham, AL, Birmingham's January was a typical Cincinnati January and Cincinnati experienced what was normal for Minneapolis.

One of the worst freezes to hit Jacksonville was the Christmas Freeze of 1983. The temperature dropped to 11 degrees on a weekend when many residents were out of town or at parties. Not hearing the weather forecasts caused many residents to wake up to frozen pipes. If they were out of town, rising temperatures a few days later caused broken pipes to flood the home's interiors. Even though this freeze was the coldest of the 20th century, a colder one occurred the following winter.

On January 21, 1985, an all-time record low of 7 degrees occurred. But residents were forewarned because it happened on a workday when people normally heard the daily weather reports. As I walked to my classroom at Jacksonville University that morning, the temperature was a bitter 12 degrees. The first thing I told the class to remember was that this morning is so cold that if they spent the rest of their lives in Jacksonville, they would never experience a day this cold again.

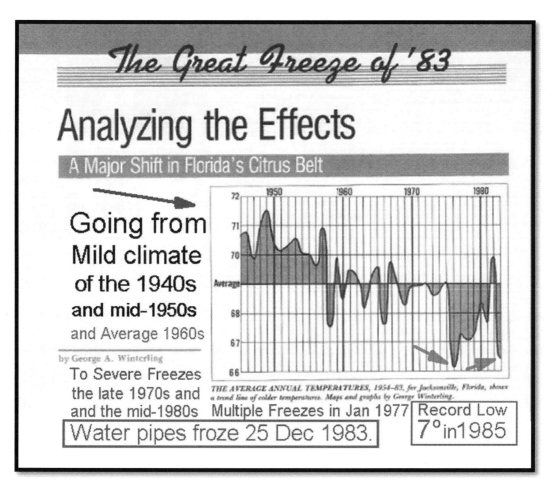

The Great Freeze of '83

Analyzing the Effects

A Major Shift in Florida's Citrus Belt

Going from Mild climate of the 1940s and mid-1950s and Average 1960s

by George A. Winterling

To Severe Freezes the late 1970s and and the mid-1980s

Water pipes froze 25 Dec 1983.

Multiple Freezes in Jan 1977

Record Low 7° in 1985

THE AVERAGE ANNUAL TEMPERATURES, 1954–83, for Jacksonville, Florida, shows a trend line of colder temperatures. Maps and graphs by George Winterling.

I had moved to the Beauclerc section of Jacksonville because of the nice neighborhood and because of its location with regard to the St. Johns River. Severe winter freezes can be moderated by the wide St. Johns River along its waterfront. The western side of the river may have temperatures in the middle 20s, while properties only a block or two east of the river may be only a couple of degrees below freezing. But with temperatures in the teens and winds 10 to 20 mph, precautions had to be taken to protect exposed pipes and tender plants in places along the St. Johns River eastern shore.

With freezes like the ones in 1983 and 1985, I had to assemble a temporary "shed" over and around my exposed citrus trees. In fact, the soil heat inside the shelter was not enough to keep the trees from freezing. I had to run water sprinklers inside the enclosures to provide additional heat.

CHAPTER 35 - Extreme Weather – Rain and Snow

When it came to reporting local rains and floods, I first became aware of Black Creek flooding around May 2, 1964. Ernie Mynatt, who lived by Doctors Lake, was a teenage weather watcher who reported 7 inches of rain that was causing heavy flooding in the Middleburg area. Ernie was a faithful reporter rainfall in this area until he graduated from high school and moved to Texas. I was shocked to learn that this promising young man was shot and killed by a robber where he worked.

Growing up in Jacksonville, I was well acquainted with the places in the city that flooded during heavy thunderstorms. The McCoy Boulevard and the Myrtle Street Underpasses below the railroad always had water ranging from one to three feet deep. On Myrtle Street, the overhead clearance of less than 10 feet often smashed the tops of trucks whose drivers failed to heed the danger signs. Several downtown corners like Clay and Adams Streets and Laura and Beaver collected enough water to threaten adjacent buildings. College Street in Riverside flooded all the way to the Foremost Dairy near Roosevelt Blvd. Many Murray Hill streets were so much lower than adjacent properties that they turned into rivers or storm drains. In the 1950s, the Sandalwood subdivision was one of the first new areas where residents discovered they faced drainage problems during heavy downpours.

On the night of May 19-20, 1959, downtown Jacksonville and San Marco had up to 15 inches of rain that submerged cars up to rooftops at the State Board of Health near Hogans Creek, The roof of a downtown furniture store collapsed from the weight of the water.

In 1964, the heaviest rain from Hurricane Dora fell well west of the city where extreme amounts of 17 and 23 inches of rainfall were recorded at Live Oak and Mayo respectively. The worst flooding I witnessed was the 200-year flood in April 1973 when the Suwannee River crested at a record 40 feet at White Springs and closed Interstate 75 as the crest passed.

Freezing rain seldom occurs in Jacksonville. The first recorded event was on January 4, 1879, when sleet turned to freezing rain at 8:30 PM. Ice continued to form on trees, wires, and shrubs until 9:30 AM on the 5th leaving a thick coating of ice. Eighty-three years later, on January 11-12, 1962 nearly 16 hours of freezing rain caused Jacksonville's worst glaze storm.

On the evening of December 22, 1989, rain started turning to ice on bridges. It turned to sleet during the night and to snow off and on during the day of the 23rd when afternoon temperatures were 26 degrees. The Hart and Dames Point bridges were closed for 4 days. While the official snow for Jacksonville was less than an inch, winds caused drifts several inches deep in sheltered places. Fernandina received nearly 2 inches, and across the state line in Georgia, Folkston had up to 5 inches.

A surprising non-rain event occurred in Jacksonville on April 30, 1971. The bright morning sunshine gave way to a darkening overcast that made the city dark as night. Street lights came on and the birds went to roost. There was no thunder or lightning, but an eerie quiet fell over the city. The National Weather Service issued a tornado warning for our area. I quickly handed our telecine operator a Tornado Warning slide, and since there was no one in the announcer's booth, I turned the switch to "on air" to broadcast the information. Oddly enough, after nearly one-half hour of darkness, daylight returned with no thunder, lightning or rain!

Over the years, northeast winds occasionally surprise Jacksonville Beach residents with torrential downpours of 5 to 10 inches, while people living away from the coast have little or no rain and are unaware of their neighbors' flooded streets. Flood waters at the beaches often cannot drain through sewers into the ocean because the streets were lower than the wind-driven higher tides of the ocean. The only way water could drain was towards the Intracoastal Waterway. In 1985 on Labor Day weekend, parts of northeast Florida along the St. Johns River were drenched with a 20-inch rainfall. On October 10, 1989, low lying St. Augustine had up to 16 inches of rain in about 5 hours.

In 1989, three days after hurricane Hugo bypassed Florida and struck Charleston, SC, a front stalled over Jacksonville and dumped torrents of rain on downtown Jacksonville. A total of 11.40 inches fell in 5 hours. There were two deaths caused by persons who mistook water-filled ditches for streets and drove right into them. In 1991, many neighborhoods in Mandarin and Orange Park were flooded from 12 to 15 inches of rain around October 1. One Beauclerc street in Pickwick Park that normally didn't flood had water deep enough to float a boat because drainage ditches were clogged with debris that even contained a discarded mattress.

In August 2008, Tropical Storm Fay came up the Florida peninsula and stalled over the east central Florida near Cape Canaveral, dumping 27.65 inches of rainfall on Melbourne. The upstream waters of the St. Johns River around Sanford received up to 18 inches of rain. Northeast Florida runoffs caused the St. Johns River to expand from its banks to virtually all low ground areas from central Florida to Jacksonville. Since the river flows northward, the water drainage to the Atlantic Ocean is constricted by the narrow gap between the river banks in the downtown Jacksonville. Our city was originally called Cowford because cattle were herded across the river at this point. Much of the northeast Florida counties also were flooded from 12 inches of rain.

Four years later, on June 24-27, 2012 Tropical Storm Debby stalled over the northeast Gulf of Mexico south of Tallahassee. While the storm's center swirled over the steamy Gulf waters for two and a half days, shearing upper-level westerly winds ripped water-laden clouds over northeast Florida causing 15 to 20 inches of rain. Rivers such as the Suwannee, St. Marys at Macclenny and Black Creek in Middleburg crested near all-time record levels; in fact, the St. Marys crested at a record 24.4 feet (12.4 feet above flood stage) on June 28. Jacksonville's peak wind from Debby, downgraded to a Depression, was only 35 mph.

The hurricane season of 2017 brought unprecedented flooding to large parts of Texas, Florida and Puerto Rico. Our (Northeast FL – Southeast GA) problem was the combination of nor-easter winds, exceptionally high tides from the solar-lunar phases, coastal and lowland development, and widespread heavy rainfall from Hurricane Irma that drenched the entire state from the Atlantic and Gulf coasts into southeastern US. Hurricane Harvey in eastern Texas produced historical rainfall - totals up to 60 inches. It will take many years for Puerto Rico to recover from the double whammy hit from Hurricanes Irma and Maria.

CHAPTER 36 - Extreme Weather – Hot

Jacksonville's official highest recorded temperature was 104 degrees on July 28, 1872, July 21,1942, and July 7, 1954.

The one-hundred-degree mark is usually not reached during many summers because the rising inland heat is often replaced with a cooling sea breeze from the Atlantic Ocean, or because of the cooling effect of convective clouds and scattered afternoon showers.

Heat waves usually affect our area when the atmosphere is extremely dry and a westerly breeze blocks the coastal seabreeze. One of the hottest days occurred in 1954 on June 28 when the mercury hit 103 degrees.

The most extreme heat waves on record occurred during the summers of 1980 and 1981. On July 11, 12 and 13, 1980 the temperatures were 100, 102 and 102 respectively. The following summer was even hotter.

The heat wave started on July 11, 1981, with 100 degrees, followed by 101 on the 12th and 13th, 102 on the 14th, 15th and 16th. The 103 degrees reached on July 17, 1981, was our hottest since 1879.

This heat wave broke all records for the most 100's in one year. Two other years topped one hundred. The temperature reached 102 degrees on July 20, 1985, and 102 again on July 31, 1999.

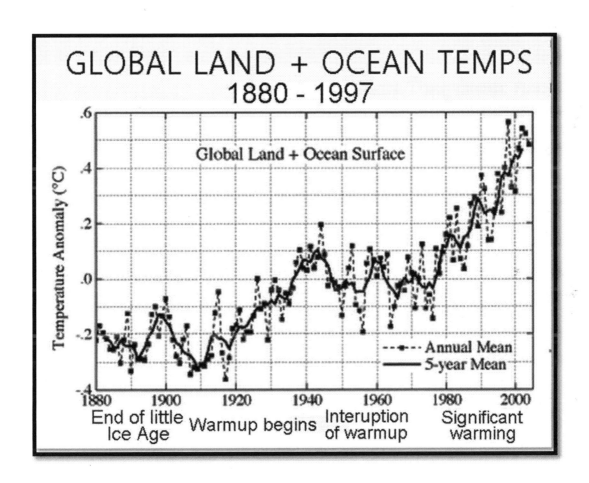

In the late 1960's, we bought a Ford Station Wagon with plans to travel to Six Flags in Atlanta with the Willis (Bill and Arie) family trailing behind. Before we reached Lake City, our radiator hose burst and we had to pull off to the side of Interstate 10 three miles short of the U.S. Highway 441 exit. The Willises stopped at the Gulf station and informed the mechanic of our problem. Surprisingly, he temporarily fixed the leak by stuffing a piece of cloth in the hole and wrapping it with a rag so enough water could remain in the radiator 'til we pulled into the station. Arriving in Atlanta, all of our kids enjoyed the rides at Six Flags.

A month or two later we drove to Lion Country Safari in south Florida, a few miles west of West Palm Beach. We were confined to the safety of our car while the animals roamed freely outside. Our air conditioner did not adequately keep us cool. When we returned home we discovered that the hot water hose from the radiator had not been turned off. It was warming the heater coils inside the car. Our travel was not as hot as we extended our travel on the Gulf coast and Sapelo Island.

We then visited Ft. Myers and the Thomas Edison Estate. I was impressed with the numerous plants growing where he was researching a source that could be used to develop rubber. He found the Goldenrod had some potential, but he was too old to finish the project.

After working five summers with the U.S. Weather Bureau in Jacksonville, plus 15 years reporting summer heat at WJXT, I realized that not all 90 degree days felt the same. When the humidity was low, it didn't feel as hot as when the humidity was higher. As a meteorologist, I was aware of the fact that the evaporation of moisture from our skin is nature's cooling mechanism. Humid air makes it more difficult for the skin's evaporation to cool the body. After studying the work of Orville Heavener, who coined the word humiture, I modified his scale to our eastern U.S. humidity.

Since the moisture content of the air is reported by the dew point temperature, I recognized that a dewpoint of 65 separated the muggy from the crisp feeling in the air. As a result, I used a simplified method to report the humiture/heat index by adding each degree that the dew point was above 65 to the temperature.

Here's an example of using the dew point and temperature to determine the humiture/heat index:

If the dew point is 75, I subtract 65 and add the 10-degree difference to the temperature. If the temperature is 90 degrees, the additional ten degrees tells us that it feels like 100.

CHAPTER 37 - Professional Outreach and Travels

I became a member of the American Meteorological Society when I became a member of the USAF Air Weather Service in the early 1950s. The AMS Bulletin was a publication that shared advances in the field of meteorology, and the Magazine, "Weatherwise," had articles on significant weather events and monthly or annual summaries related to weather or climate. Upon becoming a Broadcast Meteorologist at WJXT, I applied for the AMS television Seal of Approval. A recording of my reporting was sent to each of the five members of the AMS Board on Radio and Television Weathercasting. They, plus a selection of local AMS members, graded my broadcasts for high informational and educational value and beneficial service in keeping with standards established by the Society. In May 1963 I received the 43rd Seal issued since the program was initiated in 1957.

GEORGE WINTERLING 1972

During my first five years at Channel 4, one of my main projects was developing animations with a Kodak Cine-Special camera that had a lever for shooting single-frames. By positioning the camera over a platform that had photo lamps, I could move weather features manually, and they would move with a natural motion in the film projector.

I soon added music to a few animations and displayed them at the AMS 2nd Weathercasting Conference held in Tampa, FL in 1967.

Those attending were amazed at such movies since TV weather at that time usually consisted of a static map of the U.S. showing fronts and weather data. Around that time a company created animations of sun rays and rain showers by assembling polarized reflectors on the map. A filter rotated in front of the studio light causing apparent motions in the reflector.

1972 Mayor Hans Tanzler reads Weather Guide

In 1972, I solicited films of weather shows from AMS members. I showed these films at an AMS meeting in New Orleans. Afterwards, I sent a large reel containing more than 15 weather programs to the AMS Headquarters in Boston hoping it would be part of their archives. Years later when I inquired about them, none was found.

In 1973, as Chairman of the AMS Weathercasting Committee, I sought to improve the TV display of the AMS Seal of Approval. After soliciting suggestions from the Board, I designed the one that was adopted through the efforts of my successor, Chairman Jim Smith of WXYZ Detroit.

My television career took me to annual conferences in numerous locations across the country from San Diego, Los Angeles and Disneyland in California to places like Minneapolis, Chicago, and Boston. After the Boston meeting, veteran broadcaster Don Kent and his wife, Miriam, took us to Boothbay, ME where we enjoyed eating Maine lobster at the docks. The Committee's 25th Anniversary was held in Honolulu where my wife, Virginia, and I flew on a 700-mile three-stop tour of the Hawaiian Islands.

During the week we spent there, we visited the Polynesian Cultural Center and the sunken battleship Arizona. Other places we enjoyed visiting were Snowbird, the Mormon Tabernacle Temple in Salt Lake City, the Gateway Arch in St. Louis, the Riverwalk and Superdome Events in New Orleans and the Weather Channel in Atlanta.

Climate - Change Conference
George Winterling with Vice President Al Gore
Ocotber 1, 1997

Over the years, several of my colleagues noticed that the Conferences had changed in several ways. The first that was pointed out was that weather reporting was becoming more in terms of computer models, rather than the conventional descriptions of weather systems and their behavior. Computerized weather did not seem to be weather as we had visualized through weather charts and analysis. It appeared to us as being more abstract, being lost in the differing computer models. The second difference was the growth in the number of vendors.

The development of computer graphics had exploded. Instead of meeting to learn about our first love, the weather, we had to learn how to operate the different computer systems. Our Conferences included critiques and suggestions from several consultants.

I was surprised to learn that my weather programs and reputation were mentioned as an example of what a weather program should contain. At one of my first Conferences, I often heard consultants say to remember the KISS method, Keep It Simple Stupid.

There were memorable family trips as well. In 1976, I drove my wife, Virginia, and our daughter, Wendy, in our Ford Granada up I-75 and Canadian highway 401 to an AMS meeting in Toronto. On the day that the brand new CN tower opened, we rode the elevator to the observation level as a thunderstorm passed over the city. We drove back to the U.S. where we viewed Niagara Falls and spent the night at the Holiday Inn by the falls. We then drove to New Jersey where we spent the night in a motel in Lakewood, NJ.

After eating breakfast in Toms River, we visited Pine Beach where my brother and I were born. The large house was vacant and the parts of the picket fence had collapsed. I remembered watching my grandfather twenty years earlier mixing concrete and pouring it into molds for the posts. I picked up one of the posts and placed it in the trunk of my car for a memorial at my house. I walked into the Lamp Post Inn and inquired if anyone remembered my grandfather who had built the establishment. No one knew about him!

We then drove about 18 miles farther south to my maternal grandparent's homestead in Mayetta, now owned by my uncle and aunt, Clinton and Eleanor Cranmer. We watched my uncle hoe potatoes in his garden and went inside to talk with my aunt. We spent a few days catching up on our lives. I was particularly interested in learning more about my father who had taken his life when my brother and I were teenagers. The main thing I learned was that he was a very nice man. After leaving Mayetta, we spent the night in Washington, D.C. and visited Williamsburg, Virginia before returning to our home in Jacksonville.

In 1998, we flew to St. Louis with our granddaughter, Sarah. We rode the elevator in the Gateway Arch and Sarah enjoyed the Museum exhibit of the Lewis and Clark Expedition. She had just played the role of Sacagawea, the Indian guide, in her school play. Returning home, we saw smoke covering the Okefenokee Swamp and much of northeast Florida.

This was the El Nino year where a rainy winter produced a lot of vegetation that turned very flammable in the spring drought. The first thunderstorms of the summer season had ignited multiple wildfires.

The year of 1999 started with a New Year's trip to Tempe, Arizona, and the Fiesta Bowl. Although FSU lost to Tennessee, Virginia and I enjoyed taking our granddaughter Sarah to the southern rim of the Grand Canyon, stopping near Flagstaff where there was snow on the roadside to snap her picture. We had to wait six hours for our return flight to arrive in Phoenix due to fog in California. Consequently, we were too late to catch our connecting Delta flight in Dallas. After spending the night in Dallas hotel, we returned to Jacksonville and Sarah missed a day of school.

CHAPTER 38 - Making Community Contacts

During my broadcasting career, I enjoyed getting to see weather from the perspective of various users of the forecasts. In the 1970s, I got to go fishing in the Atlantic about 6 miles offshore with George Bull. He was fishing for tarpon, as were several other boats at the time. Suddenly, we saw a few people in the water where their boat had sunk. As they were soon rescued by other fishermen, we learned that they had started their engine to go to another location, but forgot to raise their anchor. The line simply yanked their boat underwater. A few hours later, a thunderstorm that was inland crossed the coast and heavy rains fell like a dark curtain, soon drenched us while churning the sea with waves up to five feet. I enjoyed the experience, confident that Captain Bull would return us to Mayport safely.

In 1975 during one of my speaking engagements, I met Dr. Steve Browder, Head of the Physics Department at Jacksonville University (JU). He informed me that the Department had a meteorology class that was lacking a teacher. Upon learning that I had a Bachelor of Science degree from Florida State University, he asked me to teach the class at JU. I immediately accepted since I often thought of my profession as being one informing and educating the public about the weather. I had the pleasure of meeting hundreds of aspiring students for the next 17 years, sharing films, slides and my experiences in the world of weather. Consequently, I crossed paths with dozens of them in the community during the latter part of my broadcasting career.

Around 1980, I met Rick Hendrix at Paxon Field on Jacksonville's Westside one morning as he removed a large basket and gas cylinders from his trailer. After spreading out a large balloon and placing the cylinders into the attached basket, we climbed inside and he ignited gas burners to fill the balloon with hot air. After a couple of minutes, the balloon lifted us across the field and over Woodstock Park, then across Riverside about 3,000 feet above the Fuller Warren Bridge. We had no sensation of motion. I felt like the basket was stationary and that I was just seeing the landscape below me move westward around 15 mph. Rick saw that we were drifting towards the sand dunes next to Southside Blvd, so he reduced the heat from the gas burners so that we soon had an abrupt stop on the soft ground.

A few years later, I received a call from Dr. William Clarke asking me if I would like to go soaring in his glider. I told him I always loved flying and that I would be delighted to go with him. We met at Herlong Field along Normandy Blvd on Jacksonville's Westside. When we climbed inside, he showed me the altimeter and the indicator that would tell us if we were gaining or losing altitude. After a tow plane taxied in front of us, we gradually picked up speed across the field and were carried into the air above the pine trees. We must have risen a couple thousand feet before he pulled a lever to detach the tow line. He told me that he would observe the puffy cumulus clouds because they would have updrafts under them. As we circled under one large cloud, the green light indicator let us know that we were gaining altitude. We were soon soaring to an altitude of 3,000 feet. As we drifted away from that cloud the red light told us that we were losing altitude until we found another cloud to give us a green light. Within 15 or 20 minutes we had maneuvered three or four miles farther east over the St. Johns River and part of downtown.

After flying with Dr. Clarke for about a half hour, we started to return to Herlong Field. I was surprised when he asked me if I would like to take the controls. When I did, we were under a large gray cloud that gave us an updraft that kept lifting us above 3,000 ft. A few raindrops splashed on the windshield as he told me to push to control stick forward enough to slowly descend. He then said that we were going to land at Herlong and to turn and bank into a descending spiral. I thought he would soon take over the controls, but he kept directing all the way down to the landing approach. He finally took over the controls as we came within 500 feet of the field.

In the Field of Medicine, I have met many dedicated professionals.

I met Michael Aubin, FACHE, through the Neonatal Intensive Care Unit (NICU) at Wolfson Children's Hospital. He was named Hospital President for Wolfson Children's Hospital in 2011. When my grandson's wife experienced a premature birth of her first baby, I visited the Neonatal nursery. I was impressed with the meticulous care given by the doctor and nurses. We had to scrub our hands for 3 minutes to enter the nursery.

Virginia and I had met Mr. Aubin's predecessor, Larry Freeman, when our second child was less than one year old and an inpatient at Wolfson. In the 34 years that he was the administrator of Wolfson Children's Hospital, he presided over the facility's growth from a wing of Baptist Medical Center to a 180-bed regional children's hospital serving children with critical medical needs from around the country and more than 40 countries.

Over the past 50 years, I have personally driven to dozens of communities within 100 miles of Jacksonville, and have talked with hundreds of thousands of ordinary people from all walks of life. Every time I visited a civic club, like Kiwanis or Rotary, I enjoyed discussing recent storms and weather events. I learned a lot about them and their community service. In the 1970s, our Station Manager, Bob Schellenberg, invited me to give a talk at the Green Turtle Restaurant in Jacksonville. When I heard the motto and principles of Rotary, I was always impressed with goals for living that they strived to achieve.

Through the Rotary Club in Crescent City, John Newbold allowed me to help the community raise funds for scholarships. I've watched that small community struggle for recognition because of its being so distant from large population centers. Nevertheless, their Catfish Festival parade has drawn numerous participants, such as Police and Firemen, from surrounding counties and even as far north as Jacksonville, which is 80 miles away. I was honored to be their Official Meteorologist for more than 20 years, monitoring a rain gauge for storm insurance and by joining in their annual Catfish parade.

I remain grateful for the many Keys to the City presented me by such small towns and big cities all over northeast Florida and southeast Georgia. And I am humbled by the Distinguished Alumni recognitions from Jacksonville University. I was honored to be chosen a member of the Fellow of the American Meteorological Society that presented me with their Outstanding Service Award for Public Education and Development of Weather Animation.

I have also benefited from networking with notable broadcast meteorologists such as Neil Frank and Bryan Norcross and community leaders in a multitude of Jacksonville civic organizations including a myriad of Churches, the Woman's Club of Jacksonville, and the Garden Club. In knowing all these people, I've been truly blessed.

CHAPTER 39 - Innovation and Animations

My first experience with film animation was when I purchased a Sears Tower 8mm movie camera. It had a shutter lever on it to snap single frames on a roll of movie film. I found it fascinating that I could set the camera on a tripod, point it towards the horizon and make a time-lapse movie of cloud motions by repeating "one-two-three click". After doing this for 10 or 15 minutes, the movie showed dramatic motions in the sky. When I joined Channel 4, I found a Kodak Cine-Special 16 mm camera that had been used by the Sports Department that also had a small lever to snap single frame pictures. I soon spent 30 to 45 minutes each day taking "one-two-three click" movies with the camera mounted on a tripod at different locations. I could get one of the quickest views of the sky by carrying the tripod and camera up a ladder to the roof of the Channel 4 building, but I often could catch better scenes and clouds motions by setting up at various locations along the river or at different towns, like Waycross, Lake City or Palatka.

I also could mount the camera on a Polaroid stand, that had four photo lamps for filming indoors. I devised a way to animate weather features maps by cutting out fronts and various weather features from colored art paper. By placing them on a piece of glass over the weather map, I could then push the glass bit by bit, taking a picture for each motion so that the film would contain images of things moving by themselves. Prior to each weathercast, I had to send the film to someone like Joe Burnsed for processing, then hand it over to someone like Audrey Dyer in the Telecine Department to run while I was doing the weather.

I occasionally used the glass over the U.S. Drought map to show the fire danger areas. I would simply take a can of lighter fluid, pour a bit of the liquid on the glass over the drought, light it with a match and keep clicking the camera. To study the jet stream and upper winds, I would enhance the features of each day's fax charts so I could animate the monthly and seasonal changes in the weather patterns. This process showed how a hurricane could be picked up and carried away in the westerly winds. In 1967 I made one film that I hand-delivered to the Weather Bureau's Regional Office in Fort Worth.

Around 1970, we had a special fax machine where we could dial-up pictures from remote weather stations. I made a color transparent overlay for each station and could make a movie from multiple pictures of radar echoes. These were the days before Character Generators, or Chirons, for posted words and letters. The Art Department could print white numbers on black paper. I cut them out individually to shoot a Polaroid slide of the current temperature, humidity, wind etc. that I gave to Telecine (the projector room) for the Director to display in the weather show.

In the 1970s, film cameras were being replaced with Sony video cameras. This made time-lapse photography more difficult. I had to record a 30 or 40-minute movie of the sky, and then go to an edit suite, copying two frames out of every 20 onto another tape which could be played as a "fast-motion" picture. While we had used paper maps on the weather set in the studio for almost 20 years, it was a huge adjustment when we got our first Colorgraphic computer in 1980. While maps could be constructed in the computer, we had to devise methods of overlaying movies, or events, on top of the map. We could select cities to display temperatures. Occasionally, the data received through a modem would have a glitch, or error, that we could not see until we were doing the live broadcast. I was surprised during my broadcast one January day to see the temperature for Tallahassee pop up as 135 degrees!

The illustrations of weather phenomena like hurricanes, hailstorms, and floods had to be constructed differently from the art supplies I had used, but after months of experimentation, I was able to continue to create weather animations on the computer. Several years later, my index finger started locking in the joint from repeated mouse operations. I went to an orthopedic surgeon, who informed me that I had "trigger finger", a locking of the joint. He cured it by injecting latex around the bone. I could then create my graphics with no difficulty.

In January 1984, I was given the Award for Outstanding Service by a Broadcast Meteorologist by the American Meteorological Society. From Channel 4's new tower camera, I recorded time-lapse pictures of the sky with different kinds of weather. I added appropriate music for each sequence and showed it at the national A.M.S. Broadcasters meeting in Chicago.

In 1987, the AMS honored me by electing me Fellow of the American Meteorological Society. Having been asked to research weather-related accidents for several attorneys over the years, I applied for and passed the AMS Board requirements to be a Certified Consulting Meteorologist in 1989. In 1990, Jacksonville University presented me with their Distinguished Alumni Award.

CHAPTER 40 - Computers and TV Weather

In 1977, I met with AMS meteorologists Peter Leavitt (WSI), Mark Eubank (SLC) and Elliott Abrams (Penn State) at the University of Wisconsin for a seminar on computers. We learned of the McIdas computer and of the early stages of computer graphics. Terry Kelly, a local broadcaster was in the process of developing Colorgraphics. I became acquainted with the difference between software and hardware. This was very useful in diagnosing problems when WJXT got our first computer in 1980. We received our weather data (temperatures and satellite images) through a telephone modem. The Colorgraphics software determined how the computer would transfer the signal to images and weather data.

There were several surprises when we started using the computer live on TV. Sometimes the data was faulty causing the computer to freeze. Our first computer only had 15 or 16 different colors. There was not enough memory on the hard drive for many images, so we used commands to enter the numbers on the map. A glitch in the phone signal would occasionally cause some unrealistic temperatures. A command to fill a certain polygon on the map with a color during the broadcast would find a broken border of the polygon that caused the color to spill out, filling all open areas that had no boundaries.

In the late 70's, I flew to WGN Chicago to meet with John Coleman and Joe D'Leo who were planning a national weather channel. I, along with a few other meteorologists, met after the station signed off around midnight to make a demonstration tape of this significant venture. Around 1980, John informed me that Landmark Corporation had decided to finance the channel. My wife, Virginia, and I flew to their new facility in Atlanta and witnessed how this was a monumental achievement.

In discussing the operation of the Weather Channel, I told John that I thought that it needed more than just maps, radar and satellite images. I suggested using a lot of video of actual weather would relate more to viewers who were not meteorologically savvy. Surprisingly, he saw no need for that.

While Channel 12 had always operated a weather radar for many years, we were more comfortable with using the National Weather Service radars. They had one to the north of Waycross, Georgia and one to the south in Daytona Beach. With these radars, we had no problem with ground clutter that obscured data near the radar site. We also had no equipment to maintain and update. We paid for a dedicated telephone connection to both sites, stored the images on tape via a Scott time-lapse box and were able to show the movement of the weather systems. We also had a dial-up fax system that we used to select images from other parts of the U.S.

Over the years, we discovered there was sometimes a difference between actual weather and the virtual (not real) weather as displayed by computer; in fact, its portrayal can actually be false. Around 2002, we tried My-Cast. It was so bad because it was showing our skies as overcast or raining when our skies were actually blue because the seabreeze had pushed our clouds and rain well to the west of the city. It used the MM5 forecast model. We learned that the WSI (Weather Services International) GFS and NAM weather simulations usually didn't show our hyper-local weather. The rain display had been completely misleading when it comes to showing rainfall totals. A classic example was on August 23, 2005, when it showed less than an inch of rain in the Mandarin section of Jacksonville when over 2 inches had fallen.

Before the computer, I could easily write and draw on the weather maps with a Magic Marker, but after 1981 my attempts to use the computer's telestrator were fruitless. The drawing either did not follow my motions, or the lines were too thin or faint to be of use. It took 30 years for WJXT to finally get a computer that would work properly. Upon seeing it on the screen, I promptly sent an e-mail of congratulations to Chief Meteorologist John Gaughan.

When it came to using the Hand Tracker (where you control actions on the screen by touching the screen), it was finally developed to near perfection in 2012, as illustrated by John's very efficient use of it. When we first tried it, it often didn't operate properly causing either a distraction or delay in our description of the weather. In 2012, the use of radar had been greatly enhanced as we could quickly zoom to local close-up neighborhood weather as well as sweeping moves to many other weather features. Finally, the listing of times and communities were easily legible, not in a micro-font that was barely legible.

CHAPTER 41 - Benefits of Healthful Living

I felt fortunate to have passed my 80th birthday on September 1, 2011. As a youngster, I was always concerned with being physically fit. I was often walking through trails in the woods or riding my bicycle a mile or two every day. I mowed many of my neighbor's lawns with an old push mower. I was encouraged to exercise by reading about Charles Atlas in magazines. His articles said that he was once a 97-pound weakling, but by using "Dynamic Tension" he grew into a strong, muscular adult. I read every Superman comic book I could find, thinking that I could do some of his feats. I even tied a towel behind my back, climbed to the roof of my garage and jumped off into the flower bed below. As a Boy Scout, I went camping and earned merit badges by hiking several miles and using all of the various swimming strokes. As a student at Robert E. Lee High School, I didn't play in organized games, but after the calisthenics, I usually ran several miles around the oval track surrounding the football field for the rest of the period.

In the late 70's, I learned about aerobics and the jogging craze when I joined the choir of Jacksonville's First Baptist Church. I started building my breathing capacity by alternating running and walking a few blocks, then gradually increasing it to a full run a mile and a half from my home in Beauclerc Cove to Scott Mill Road and back. I finally built my endurance up to running a full six miles without stopping. Before long I realized that I had enough stamina to run in the city's annual 15K River Run. After participating in five races, I decided to reduce my running to about 3 miles because I felt that the wear on my knees and my spine was not good for me. I had always watched my diet by reducing meat that contained fat, and by eating vegetables daily. I didn't eliminate sweets completely, but I was careful not to overindulge. Between careful food selections at the Morrison's and Picadilly cafeterias, plus eating healthful food prepared by my wife, Virginia, I was in excellent health.

Upon reaching the age of 55, I noticed that the many years of running had caused the skin to sag on my face and neck. Upon examination by Dr. Anwar Kamal, a local plastic surgeon, I agreed to have a rhytidectomy (facelift) operation. During surgery, Dr. Kamal discovered a few skin cancers on me that he later removed. A year or two later, I discovered my eyelids had been sagging so that my peripheral vision was reduced. Unfortunately, Dr. Kamal died in 1992 having accidentally nicked himself during surgery, giving him Hepatitis B. He was a patron of the arts and had many items on display at the Cummer Art Gallery in Jacksonville.

I enjoyed running so much that I continued to enter several community and charity walks and runs; but eleven years later, I had to have another operation to correct some more sagging of the face and jowls. This time I used Dr. David Mobley who had taken over Dr. Kamal's practice.

I think our grandchildren helped keep both me and Virginia feel young. I had great pleasure in interacting with my grandchildren. My son, Frank, had two very active boys that climbed trees and were seldom idle. My son-in-law, Bob Schwank and I, built a fort from timbers that stood nearly ten feet tall that gave them a much safer way to climb. We built an attached sandbox for their sister, Sarah, to play in. Sarah played on our swing set, rode her tricycle playing Take-out (MacDonald's) and singing Christmas songs.

I always grew flowers and vegetables in my backyard garden. Before granddaughter, Amanda Schwank was two years old, she was helping me plant and appeared in my TV George's Garden films. At one time we added a playhouse to the garden and a sandbox shaped like a turtle. We also had a great time playing indoors.

Papa and his number 1 helper, Amanda

When she wasn't watching Barney and Baby Bop or Gullah-Gullah Island, we assembled puzzles like the Alphabet Train that had different animals for each letter or Lion King that had many animals from the jungle in the movie. We had a church pew on our porch with a Noah's Ark and animals. We played Bride and Groom and rode to the K-Mart for her to put 2 quarters into the slot to ride a mechanized pony. We stayed busy!

Virginia provided nutritious and delicious meals for us. Whether it was after church on Sundays, a birthday or Thanksgiving dinner, each person's favorite dish was on the table. All of the grandchildren loved her macaroni and cheese. Broccoli casserole, lima beans, brown rice and white acre peas always accompanied the mouth-watering roast beef and gravy. As the years went by, our daughter, Wendy, was invaluable in lending a helping hand. Her large bowl of Chocolate delight satisfied those of us who were chocoholics and Virginia's pecan pies, topped with Reddi-whip, topped off after dinner conversations better than any holiday football game

I had no serious medical problems. In 1967, our station manager, Jim Lynagh, suggested I see an allergist to determine the cause of my post-nasal drip. I visited Dr. Melvin Newman who tested me for tree and plant pollens. A serum was prepared for me to get 3 years of injections that would cause my body to build up my immunity to various early spring heavy tree pollens. At times over the years, I still had to use Dristan, then Contac and finally Coricidin for relief from occasional allergic reactions to the many days with high pollen counts.

CHAPTER 42 - Battle with Health

I was very health-conscious when approaching my 65th birthday in 1996. While Virginia and I were attending the AMS Weather Conference in Boston, I noticed that I felt off balance while waiting for an elevator. My doctor checked me and made a note of it, but found nothing wrong. The next year we went to Snowbird, UT for a conference in the mountains. I had no trouble jogging a mile or two in the high altitude, but Virginia became breathless climbing the steps to our hotel.

I finally got to meet Katherine Graham, publisher of the Washington Post, when she visited Channel 4. She always called WJXT her "lucky rabbit's foot" because of its outstanding success in investigative reporting and community involvement. Her father was Eugene Meyer, a New York City financier who had purchased the Washington Post at a bankruptcy sale. Her mother was of German descent, a bohemian intellectual. Katherine sadly died in 2001 after suffering from a fall on a sidewalk while visiting Sun Valley, Utah.

I was now reaching my late sixties with no serious health problems. Dr. John Baker had given me very thorough physical exams. His only suspicion occurred after 15 years earlier when he listened to my heart and thought there might be a slight problem. He referred me to a cardiologist, Dr. Paul Dillahunt, who gave me an echocardiogram and said he didn't notice anything serious.

Suddenly at the age of 67 following a prostate examination, I found myself being referred by Dr. Baker to a urologist, Dr. John Whittaker, who took around 10 biopsies and informed me that I had prostate cancer.

When I entered a clinic on Riverside Avenue for a bone scan and a CT, I was asked for what reason. It was the first time I ever had to use the word "cancer". On November 19, 1999, I had a prostatectomy at Baptist Medical Center. While recovering the next day, extreme pain in my armpits caused me to buzz the nurse who immediately gave me a nitroglycerin. A blocked artery had caused me to suffer a heart attack.

Because of my critical condition following the prostate surgery, the doctors had to wait to determine which procedure to use to bypass the blocked artery. In consultation with Dr. Paul Farrell, a surgeon, Dr. John Koster, told me that there was a 3% chance I would not survive the surgery. If I didn't have the bypass, I would be an invalid the rest of my life. I immediately told him, "Go for it!"

After two weeks in the hospital and recuperating enough to walk, I was sent home. After 24 hours, I began suffering excruciating pain. My body was swelling with fluid and I was readmitted to Baptist Hospital with congestive heart failure. After spending a week in critical care to remove the fluid, I had lost about 20 pounds and had to learn to walk again. When I could walk a distance of about 100 feet with a walker, I was sent home. I was told that to regain weight I should eat all kinds of food and sweets. I asked my cardiologist, Dr. Paul Farrell, what about my cholesterol. He said that I didn't have to worry about that right now. He said we can deal with that later.

I had been drinking a chocolate drink called Ensure at the hospital. When I got home, Virginia used it to make milkshakes with vanilla ice cream. During my recovery, the Peterbrooke Chocolate company sent me a large basket containing samples of all their chocolate candies. I then developed a routine to rebuild my strength. When I came home from the hospital, I could walk no further than from the couch to the adjacent room. I decided that I would do that each day for one minute, but doubling the distance every other day. After 10 days, I could walk the entire length of the house twice from the kitchen to the bedroom in around five minutes. By the end of the month, I increased my walking time to fifteen minutes and I was allowed to walk out the front door for the first time.

CHAPTER 43 - The 21st Century and Still Traveling

They called it Y2K, and there were many uncertainties about the effect of going from the 1900's to the 2000's in the computer era, especially in the realm of finance and banking. On January 15, my recovery from surgery was advancing where I was able to walk around our neighborhood cul-de-sac, and by mid-February, I was able to return to work at Channel 4. I could barely climb the stairway to the canteen, but after a few more weeks, my stamina allowed me to climb effortlessly. As the year progressed, I could participate in some of the community fundraisers, such as the Heart Walk and the March of Dimes walk. Finally, I could resume planting and filming George's Garden at the TV station, but unfortunately, could not attend the AMS Conference in San Francisco. Virginia and I were both sad, but I really felt bad because I had already been to a Conference there and Virginia hadn't. We had hoped Steve would accompany us both there sometime in the future.

Virginia and I enjoyed our second trip to an AMS meeting in Minneapolis. We took our granddaughter, Amanda, to let her enjoy her favorite pastime - shopping in a big city. We ate dinner one day at Ruth's Chris which was only a block from our hotel. On another day we discovered a new restaurant to add to our favorites, McCormick & Schmick's Seafood. While walking back to our hotel, we saw Bob Breck and his wife, Paula. We enjoyed catching up on our lives since the last Conference. We were shocked to learn that Paula, a 54-year-old mother and school teacher had died six months later.

While in Minneapolis, we spent a day at the Mall of America, a huge three-story building adjacent to a playground that had many rides, including a log roll and a roller coaster. It was like a compact Disneyland for Amanda, being a nine-year-old girl!

In 2002, Channel 4 had a two-year reunion of veteran employees from the years prior to 1980 at Jacksonville Beach. It was called "Four ever 4" which was a gathering that brought many nationally known reporters including Mike Patrick of ESPN and Steve Kroft of CBS 60 Minutes.

In 2003, I served on Duval County's Urban Horticultural Committee, participated in the Memorial Park 5 Mile Cancer walk with my Granddaughter Amanda and her friend, Madeline Bronson. Brad Nitz joined our weather staff, a tremendous asset. He was well-known for his reporting the 1998 central Florida tornado outbreak on February 2-3 that caused 42 fatalities.

These were my years of recording neighborhood weather. Each day, I drove to a different neighborhood or community with my camera and tripod to capture a 15-second movie of their weather. I tried to capture a type of weather that was either unique for that locale or different from that which was occurring in Jacksonville. I'd drive more than a hundred non-reimbursed miles to film things like Jekyll Island in Georgia or the sunny beach at Palm Coast, FL where a large condo was under construction, or around the smoke of a burning Okefenokee Swamp for a shot of my walking away from the community store in Fargo, GA.

A couple of times after shooting a scene in Lake City and Bryceville, I had placed my camera in the car trunk and driven about ten miles towards Jacksonville before remembering that had left my tripod at the film site. That mishap made my trip back 20 miles longer. A long round trip to Waycross or Palatka to show a brief clip of their community in my 6 o'clock weather report was boring, but I always thought it was the least I could do to connect them with our broadcast studio in downtown Jacksonville.

2003 George and Virginia in Anchorage, AK

In August 2003, Virginia and I attended the AMS Weathercasting Conference in Seattle. During a break in the Conference, we visited the Famous Space Needle and rode the "Duck", an amphibious landing craft through the city and into the Lake Union for a fabulous view of the city's shoreline. Following the Conference, we flew to Anchorage where we enjoyed seeing students performing at the Alaskan Native Heritage Center. After a few delicious Salmon dinners, we rode the train past Talkeetna to Denali Park. After spending the night in a lodge on a hill above the Park entrance, we rode a bus through the park. When the bus stopped, we were reminded not to discard anything on the Park property because it would disturb the animal's native environment. We could only see the base of the large Alaskan mountain range because of a dominant overcast during the entire trip.

We rode a van back to Anchorage with a rest stop at Talkeetna. This was the place that a few people had gotten off the train for a helicopter tour of Mt. McKinley. That mountain is over 20,000 feet high. If I ever go back there, that's what I'd like to see. I've never ridden in a helicopter, but that is one place I would try it. In Anchorage, we enjoyed a tour of some of the residential neighborhoods bordering Cook Inlet where the gigantic 1964 earthquake struck.

In 2005, Virginia and I celebrated our 50th Wedding Anniversary at Morton's Steak House. Afterwards, we flew to California to see the Creation play at the Crystal Cathedral and Disneyland. We enjoyed a brief visit to the Mall in Newport Beach.

In August, we flew to Washington, DC to attend the 34th AMS Broadcast Meteorology Conference at the Omni Shoreham Hotel. I enjoyed having lunch with Harry Volkman, who had just retired from a long broadcasting career that began in Oklahoma City and wound up in Chicago. Virginia and I toured the National Cathedral where were surprised to find our neighbors, Scott and Vicky Findley, in the gift shop, too. It was a very hot August as we visited the National Archives, the Ford Theater and the Holocaust Museum. We got into the WWII Duck amphibian vehicle and rode into the Potomac for a waterfront tour of the capital. This was my final attendance at an AMS conference.

We took another trip to California in December 2005, flying back to California with our granddaughter, Amanda. We were fortunate to witness one of the last hurrahs of the Crystal Cathedral at the Christmas pageant that had flying angels. Sadly, the church went into bankruptcy in 2010 and was finally purchased in 2012 by the Catholic Diocese of Orange County, to be renamed the Christ-Cathedral after renovation.

CHAPTER 44 - Rash of Notable Hurricanes

The year 2004 was similar to the 1940s for Florida. The first storm was Tropical Storm Bonnie on August 12. During that afternoon, tornado warnings were issued for several counties west of Jacksonville. I went outside to view the cloud formations and saw a sky unlike any that I had ever seen before. The dense cirrostratus overcast lowered to a very ominous nimbostratus on the southwestern horizon. I immediately went into the building, aimed the tower camera in that direction and started recording.

A tornado warning had been issued for Duval County and our News Director, Mo Ruddy-Baker, came to the weather desk inquiring about the situation. I told her that the National Weather Service had just canceled the tornado warning. To my surprise one of our reporters in called in from northwest Jacksonville reporting that a tornado was hitting buildings. While I had captured the clouds with the tornado faintly visible, the camera crew filmed close-up pictures of the funnel striking a church near Dunn Avenue.

The next day, on August 13, 2004, Hurricane Charley was aimed at the Tampa Bay area, but a slight jog to the east caused it to slam the Punta Gorda area with 145 mph winds. It was the first of four hurricanes that passed over Orlando that year. Three weeks later on September 4-5, the second hurricane, Frances, crossed the peninsula south of Jacksonville, causing power outages and downing many trees and tree limbs over northeast Florida. On September 26, Hurricane Jeanne was the third storm to cross the Florida peninsula. It followed the same path as Frances, adding to a number of fallen trees and limbs over northeast Florida before the waste removal trucks could clear neighborhoods of all the debris. Residents who were tired of waiting for trash collectors were greeted by an unpleasant stench at the recycling area off Phillips Highway where there was a mountainous heap of soggy decaying material.

The fourth hurricane to slam Florida was Ivan. It was a long-lasting Cape Verde storm that hit Pensacola on September 16 with a storm surge that swept as much as 20 miles inland from the beaches along some waterways. The bridges on US 90 and Interstate 10 had severe damage. It continued northward to Virginia and Delaware as an extratropical storm that turned moved southward off the Carolinas. It crossed south Florida and crossed the Gulf of Mexico, becoming a tropical storm again that made landfall in southwest Louisiana.

The hurricane season of 2005 broke the record of having the most tropical storms. The previous record was 21 in 1933. 2005 exhausted the list of alphabetical names, so it was necessary to add the use of Greek names Alpha, Beta, Gamma, Delta, Epsilon, and Zeta, to compile a list of 28 storms. Katrina formed in the Bahamas, intensified over southern Florida to become a major Category 5 hurricane in the Gulf of Mexico south of New Orleans on August 28. The northern Gulf coast was warned of possible catastrophic damage from Katrina. The center hit the Louisiana/Mississippi border as a strong Category 3 storm. A 20 to 30 feet storm surge on the Mississippi coast caused massive destruction at Biloxi and Gulfport. Severe flooding in New Orleans was not caused by the surge, but by 53 levee breaches that had contained Lake Ponchartrain and the Mississippi River. The death toll there exceeded 1,000, while total lives lost along the coast was estimated to be 1,836. It was the deadliest U.S. hurricane since the Palm Beach-Okeechobee storm of 1928.

On October 24, a strong category 2 hurricane Wilma crossed the southern tip of Florida. Five days earlier it had been a strong category 5 hurricane in the western Caribbean north of Honduras. As it approached the Atlantic, strong winds ripped sidings off one of the tall buildings in Ft. Lauderdale. The final storm of the season formed on December 30, thirty days after the official season ended. It contained tropical storm force winds in the mid-Atlantic between Africa and the Lesser Antilles until January 6.

CHAPTER 45 - Surgeries, Weddings, and a Storm Named Fay

Virginia had been experiencing back pains for nearly 15 years. In 2007, it reached the point where she was losing feeling in her left leg. An examination by Dr. Michael Scharf revealed that the cartilage between two of her vertebrae had eroded to the point where the nerves to her leg were being pinched. Being scheduled for surgery, she went to the Jacksonville Blood Bank to store some of her blood. She has very small veins and the nurse spent 45 minutes trying to draw blood from her left arm before attempting to draw it from her right arm. Her surgery had to be postponed because she developed blood clots. It took over three months for her to be cleared for surgery. She had the spinal fusion on July 3 that ultimately relieved the pain, but did little to restore the feeling.

The following year her cardiologist discovered that her aortic valve was slowly failing. She had trouble breathing after taking short walks. After an examination by Dr. Farrell on May 29, surgery was scheduled for the valve replacement on August 21. On August 11, Wendy, Amanda and Virginia flew to Chicago, one of their favorite places for shopping. She quickly tired during the trip and upon their return home.

On the Monday evening of August 18, she suffered severe pain in the back of her neck and shoulder. We took her to the Emergency room at Baptist, she went to the cath lab on Wednesday and had the valve replaced with a pig valve on Thursday, August 21. This was the day Tropical Storm Fay was slowly moving across northeast Florida dumping up to 20 inches of rain. My daughter, Wendy, and I took turns staying with her while torrential rains caused the St. Johns River to overflow and block access to the hospital during high tides. Mike and Billie Fouty had come during the surgery and recuperation. Being a retired policeman, Mike was allowed to pass through when the flooded road was closed.

At this same time, our granddaughter, Sarah, was marrying Daniel Denton. It was very unfortunate that we had to miss this important occasion in her life. We were also looking forward to the wedding of my grandson, Jeff, to Kimberly Galup on October 4. Fortunately, Virginia recovered sufficiently so that we all could attend the wedding in the Presbyterian Church in Atlantic Beach and the reception at the Casa Marina at Jacksonville Beach.

CHAPTER 46 - George's Big Secret

After serving as WJXT's Chief Meteorologist for 47 years, my latest contract would expire on May 31, 2009. I had been receiving one of the top salaries for my on-air work, and the broadcasting industry was forced to cut back because of poor economic conditions. Channel 4 was doing very well in the competition for viewers. The station had severed ties with CBS in 2002 and maintained a lead as number one in the market as an independent station. Due to technological advances, the station was able to continue to operate with a thirty or more percent reduction of employees.

In early spring, I met with News Director, Mo Ruddy-Baker, about my future. I told her that I still enjoyed my work and community activities, but that I recognized that the station could no longer afford my full-time services. The result was the station would announce that I had a "Big Secret" during the May ratings. At the end of my last 6 PM weathercast, the secret was revealed. I would become Meteorologist Emeritus, passing the torch of Chief Meteorologist to John Gaughan. I would be available for fill-in or assistance to the weather department and as Hurricane Expert would write George's Blog on JustWeather.com.

Being semi-retired didn't free me from going to the TV station most days. It was not for weather forecasting, but for continuing to maintain George's Garden and to read the WJXT rain gauge in the garden. It's important to know whether the plants are getting enough water, especially since we didn't have sufficient rainfall many times. I was disappointed when I learned that I had to continue the gardening duties, even though Denise Fox, the station's executive assistant, could also be of help to me. A few of the engineers, like Al Valentine, offered help on many occasions.

Most of the months were very dry. Virginia was upset that I had to drive to the garden almost daily, as well as weekends, to tend the plants. The water faucet was 40 feet from the garden; therefore, I either had to carry a dozen or more buckets of water to the plants or unwind a 100 ft. garden hose from the faucet to the garden. One summer day, the temperatures approached the middle and upper 90's. The heat tired me so much that I had to lie on the sidewalk where there was shade under the oak tree to cool down. On September 29, 2010, I was so fatigued that I tripped on the rolled up hose that was stored between the two bushes and landed on my left hip. Upon going into the station, I was told they wanted me on the air at 6 PM because of a weak tropical storm, Nicole, near the northern coast of Cuba. I told them that we had no reason to be concerned with it and that it would pass east of Miami. When they learned of my fall, they sent me to Solantic for an X-ray. Fortunately, it was only a bruise.

Upon watching the 5 PM News, I was shocked to hear Tom Wills say that Nicole would impact our area. I fired an e-mail to the station telling them the only rain that we were getting was from a stationary front over north Florida and that the heaviest rain from Nicole was southeast of Nicole over Jamaica. The next day, I was told that I would no longer have to come in to maintain the garden.

The task of constructing George's Blog as Hurricane Expert was a real challenge. I had to learn how to assemble the weather descriptions over satellite images, or tabulate weather data and insert them into WordPress. It disturbed Virginia that I had to spend many uninterrupted hours at the computer, analyzing weather data, answering e-mails, and assembling the Blog. In addition, my beagle, Callie, missed my attention and often begged me to take her for a walk.

After 47 years of being Chief Meteorologist, I was aware of many significant changes taking place at Channel 4. I had seen hundreds, maybe a thousand or more, fellow employees leave WJXT. Some moved on to other stations, and even to the networks. Several were employed by local hospitals or businesses. I had been providing Collard greens from George's Garden to Joyce Morgan-Danford and her family until she left to become a spokesperson for the Jacksonville Transportation Authority. I rejoiced with Nancy Rubin when she had a baby, Leah, around the same time that my daughter, Wendy, presented me with a granddaughter, Amanda. I enjoyed seeing her as Communications Director on the television weekly program JAXPORT Review.

Weather and gardening were among my many interests. I filmed my planting and harvesting for part of my weather program since I started at Channel 4 in 1962. In 1991, our Station Manager, Steve Wasserman, suggested that we have a garden outside the TV station. We showed that garden and the one I had at home twice a week. My granddaughter, Amanda, frequently appeared in the show. After 2005, I bought a beagle puppy that appeared in the garden. We named her Callie because her colors of black, brown and white were Calico. I filmed her coming out of her doggie door and following me around the yard and garden. Because of viewers' interest in Callie, we invited viewers to send pictures of their pets to show on TV for what we called "Dog Days". This was so popular that we continued showing pet pictures for two years.

While at Channel 4, I witnessed two economic downturns that resulted in staff reductions. The first was in the early 70's and the last was around 2008. Being concerned with job security in 1973, I considered returning to the security of a government career. On one occasion, I flew to the Regional Weather Bureau office in Ft. Worth between weather programs.

A year later, I met with one of my former Weather Bureau coworkers at Silver Spring, MD to apply for a position in D.C. A few months later, I was offered a job, but I declined because television seemed to be becoming more secure. Fortunately for the many faithful friends and viewers, I continued to be challenged by the task of having the most accurate and meaningful weather program possible.

The downturn in the economy around 2008 and the changes in station operations were of much concern to me and the station management. Station operations were also changing because of automation. Studio cameras were operated by remote control and jobs were reduced by multi-tasking from a central operations center. While I was still Chief Meteorologist and weather anchor for the 6 PM and 6:30 PM newscasts, more of my time was being used maintaining and filming George's Garden and representing Channel 4 at schools and club meetings. Realizing I could no longer continue to work fulltime, I was told that I could continue as Meteorologist Emeritus and work part-time.

Initially, I was expected to continue maintaining George's Garden, but after suffering two falls and injuring my hip, I was released from this activity. In 2010, my main duty was to occasionally appear on Channel 4 and to be known as Hurricane Expert, writing weather Blogs on News4Jax.com.

With so many years of active daily broadcasting behind me, Harry Reagan, former president of the Jacksonville Historical Society, contacted me about interviewing me about my years with WJXT. After attending legendary sportscaster Dick Stratton's funeral in 2005, he realized that many of Jacksonville's pioneer broadcasters were passing away without stories of the origin and progression of the media being told. With the assistance of WJXT Channel 4, he interviewed a dozen people, including Virginia Atter Keys, Norm Davis and me to include on the Jacksonville Historical Society website. After a series of informal meetings with retired broadcasters, the Jacksonville Broadcasters Association was organized in 2012.

CHAPTER 47 - Near Death Experience

On September 7, 2011, I spent the afternoon trimming bushes and cleaning out my backyard shed. I had finally taken time to discard many of the old unused items for the garbage pickup on Thursday. I had no recollection of the rest of that day, nor of the cleaning out the shed until I learned of it ten days later.

Virginia informed me that I had cooked hamburgers on the grill after taking a shower. We ate dinner together and she went to the family room to watch TV. Shortly after 10 PM, she said I suddenly dropped to the floor in front of her leaving Callie with her leash still on. I was not breathing and had no pulse. She immediately called 911 on the house phone and used her cell phone to call my daughter Wendy, who lives behind us. Her husband Bob Schwank, arrived within a minute to administer CPR. I learned later that he was trained in it, but this was the first time he used it. Rescue Unit and Fire Truck arrived a couple of minutes later to take over treatment and transport me to the hospital. They radioed ahead to alert Baptist Medical Center of my immediate arrival.

After putting me on a ventilator and taking me through the cath lab, it was determined that part of my brain was being damaged by lack of oxygen. A stent was placed in one of my arteries, and my body was chilled to 32 degrees Celsius to reduce further damage. I was unconscious for five days and five days later was released for rehab at Brooks Rehabilitation Hospital. Fortunately, I wasn't weakened as severely as with my first heart attack and congestive heart failure. With a weakened and damaged heart, I had to curtail strenuous activities and reduce my yard work to light gardening and guiding a self-propelled lawn mower and electric edger to keep our lawn trimmed.

Upon visiting my cardiologist, Virginia and I discussed my ability to continue driving my car. Dr. Farrell said I was physically able to drive, but the Florida Department of Transportation would not approve. Before we left, we met Dr. Hassel, who was on duty the night I was brought to the hospital. Channel 4 had not reported on my medical emergency because Virginia and Wendy thought it was a private affair. Finally, because of a barrage of public inquiries, we allowed them to do a report in November. Mary Baer talked with Dr. Hassel about the event, I met with the Rescue 911 unit at Fire Station 51, and both Anchors Tom Wills and Mary Baer came to our house to recreate the incident.

I appeared on the Morning Show to describe my condition and the changes I had to make. I described my implanted Cardioverter-defibrillator and how I had to avoid close contact with electromagnetic fields like those in cell phones and electric motors. I had a monitor by my bed that sent heart information to my cardiologist. I was reminded to call 911 if the Defibrillator was activated. One of my biggest adjustments was to stop driving. The fact that my heart could stop without notice made it necessary that I allow someone else to drive out of concern for pedestrians and other drivers.

In 2012, WJXT recognized me for my 50 years of service to the station and to the community. A one hour Special* program was aired on June 11, 2012, which was fifty years to the day that News Director, Bill Grove and Station Manager, Glen Marshall, hired me. Special Sports Director Sam Kavouris, interviewed my son, Steve Winterling, Head Baseball Coach at Pasco-Hernando Community College and News Anchor, Mary Baer, traveled to Tallahassee to interview my granddaughter, Amanda Schwank, now a junior at Florida State University. Amanda had appeared in my George's Garden shows from when she was less than two to five years old. Veteran News Anchor Tom Wills interviewed me about the innovations that I had introduced to TV during my career.

Fellow News Anchor, Rob Sweeting, had an experience similar to mine in 1999 at Baptist Medical Center. In 2004, his heart attack was treated by the same nurse and in the same room by Fe (Fay) Tanalgo, RN. Not only did I have many memories of the past five decades for the Special, I had collected more than a thousand pictures and several mementos. Anchor of *The Morning Show*, Bruce Hamilton, came to my house for a display of my photo albums. My wife, Virginia, always had told me to "get rid of that junk". It may have outlived its usefulness, but I'm writing my memories in this My

143

Life Journal and at the urging of Harry Reagan, former president of the Jacksonville Historical Society, hope to leave it with my "junk" at the Jacksonville Historical Society.

CHAPTER 48 - End of a Career

After nearly 60 years of driving, my heart condition made it unsafe for me to be behind the wheel on roadways. Fortunately, the love of my life, Virginia, was five years younger than me and was still able to be my designated driver. We coordinated our schedules so she was available to drive me to meetings, appointments, and stores. I had enough interests and hobbies centered around our home, family and the computer that I found it relatively easy to adjust to a more confining lifestyle.

Not being readily available to appear on TV during storm emergencies, Channel 4 came to my home for broadcasts, either by a remote broadcast or by telephone. By using my computer and the internet, I tracked storms that threatened our area. With WJXT's News4Jax.com website Weather/Hurricane tab, the public was informed of my analysis storm situations.

With only two years left on my part-time contract with WJXT, the 2012 hurricane season turned out to be memorable for three reasons. The first was the premature formation of two tropical systems off the southeast U.S. coast before the official beginning of the hurricane season. The second one, tropical storm Beryl, passed directly over Jacksonville on a track that resembled Jacksonville's worst hurricane Dora in 1964. Fortunately, Beryl's winds were not so destructive gusting only to 65 mph at Jacksonville Beach on the evening of May 27.

The second significant storm was tropical storm Debby which stalled over the northeastern Gulf of Mexico for more than two days. Upper-level westerly winds sheared at least three rounds of torrential rains over northeast Florida causing severe flooding along Black Creek, the St Marys, and Suwannee Rivers. The Suwannee rose to its highest crest since hurricane Dora in 1964.

The third significant storm Sandy overshadowed Isaac which caused severe flooding on the Louisiana-Mississippi coast. Hurricane Sandy headed north well east of Jacksonville Beach only causing northeaster conditions. But it interacted with a developing winter storm over the Great Lakes to send a devastating storm surge to the

New Jersey coast and New York City area. Lower Manhattan tunnels were flooded, gusty winds fanned a fire that destroyed a hundred homes at the Breezy Point borough of New York City and ripped sand dunes away into Jersey coastal communities.

The winter of 2012-13 was relatively mild and I enjoyed a Chamber of Commerce type season. The azaleas were blooming in January and the citrus began to bloom a month early in the first week of February. As expected, a brief mid-February freeze occurred, but only caused minor damage in my neighborhood because of the moderating effect of the St. Johns River. Our lawn, being serviced by TruGreen, remained truly green all winter, unlike the landscape of more inland neighborhoods west of the river.

I had finally found a spot next to my driveway to place a sapling of a unique blooming bush that my son Frank's surgeon, Dr. Fechtel, had given me in the 1970's. It's called "Yesterday Today and Tomorrow" because it keeps sprouting flowers that are purple one day, fade to pink the next day and finally white until the petals fall.

We had so many 80 degree days in January that the citrus trees were sprouting new growth a month early. I had been having only limited success in bud-grafting, the process where you can have different varieties of citrus on one tree. I had been unsuccessful in grafting my daughter, Wendy's, Red Navel buds to my Blood orange tree because that tree was older had less active buds. John Newbold, a grower in Putnam County told me that around March 1 was the best time for bud-grafting. I had limited success transferring Murcott tangerine buds to my Blood Orange trees. I wanted the tangerines on my Blood orange tree because tangerines ripen earlier than the Blood oranges which don't ripen until March. That way I could enjoy the tangerines if I lost the Blood oranges in freezes of our colder winters.

CHAPTER 49 - Memories of a Lifetime

Having spent my younger years on New Jersey's eastern shore, my interests centered both on rural life from south Jersey and the metropolitan world adjacent to north Jersey, I witnessed the 20th century growth of communication and travel as I listened to New York's Mayor Fiorello LaGuardia read the comics on the radio, studied the photo-filled New York Daily News and watched sky-writing airplanes spell Coca-Cola in the blue skies over Manhattan. Having moved to a different kind of city in northeast Florida, I saw evidence of a bygone era where there were decaying waterfront docks that once moored river-cruising steamboats. I witnessed the rails of former streetcar lines and rode in the Motor Transit Company's buses, even one that was a mini-bus that had been used at the New York World's Fair. Downtown had many historic buildings that reflected the architecture that northern cities preserved, but in the attempt to grow into a bold new city many were demolished to either showplace modern 20th century windowed structures or replaced stores and offices with a multitude of parking lots. But Jacksonville still looked to the future by building an efficient Expressway system before Eisenhower's interstate highways.

My world expanded through military service, college and government service where I enjoyed sharing life experiences with hundreds of colleagues who moved to other places, most of whom I usually saw again in my memorabilia, or with my memory. By choosing a career in broadcast meteorology that lasted more than 50 years, my life was enriched by never seeing a stranger. Everywhere I went people talked with me about their family, growing up with me and of their departed family members that always gathered in front of the TV at suppertime.

Looking back at highlights of my 50 years with WJXT, I felt honored to a part of outstanding News Anchor teams. Originally, I was part of the Evening News with News Director Bill Grove and Sportscaster Dick Stratton. Through the years, Channel 4 News had more viewers than all other local TV stations as a result of breaking investigative news reports between 1963 and 1990. Again I felt privileged to be a part of one of the nation's longest-running local news teams with Tom Wills and Deborah Gianoulis and sportscaster Sam Kouvaris.

Deborah was a co-anchor with me on Eyewitness News for 25 years. She was an excellent role model on appearance, manners and an appreciation of the value of ordinary people. And personally, she has been an exceptionally kind friend and an anchor of stability whenever I have encountered difficult events in my life.

SAM KOUVARIS   TOM WILLS   DEBORAH GIANOULIS GEORGE WINTERLING

We were together for between 1981 and 2003, at which time Deborah retired from broadcasting. The high point of our career was making a promotional film, "Snow Dreaming" in Peaceful Valley, CO. For safety sake, each of us flew to Colorado on separate flights. The pictures of our activities in the snow were a striking contrast to our local viewers in sunny Florida.

I found it strange that looking at time in the future seems much more distant than looking in the past. In many ways, it seemed that it was only a few years ago that my middle age sons and daughter were young children. While I often think of being a child with my grandparents, I see my world reversed as I have become a grandparent to my children's children. It has been an even greater blessing becoming a great-grandparent with each new child opening my eyes to the vastness of God's Wonderful World.

The fact that my father died when he was only 39 years old made it difficult for me to picture myself living past that age, and being a Christian and learning about Jesus dying at the age of 33 gave me doubts about my reaching old age. I always enjoyed having long conversations with my elders, like my wife Virginia's parents, Henry and Eunice Carter, and my mother's landlady, Louise Matthews. My relations with adults were usually with authority figures – Boy Scout counselors, school teachers, and church pastors. Many of my experiences in life were relegated to either books and encyclopedias or the great outdoors. That's where meteorology and gardening played a large part in my life experiences.

I learned a lot about life from my wife, Virginia. She was an excellent homemaker, and even though she was a bit of an introvert, she was a real people-person. I looked forward to her opinion about things and often asked for her advice. We were both perfectionists about many things and raising children was a challenge. Our boys were both more athletic than me, participating in organized sports. I enjoyed observing sports and joining the jogging/running craze of the 1980's and 90's, but I was also wide-eyed about many things in the world around me. I was interested in so many things that I found it hard to focus on one particular thing.

I was very philosophical about life, loving nature as expressed by poets like Henry Wadsworth Longfellow, Henry David Thoreau, and Joyce Kilmer. I shared King David's awe of God's creation as expressed in Psalm 19 with the "heavens declare the glory of God". Throughout my sixty years as a photographer and meteorologist, I enjoyed capturing and sharing the magnificent beauty of weather and its effect on the earth's landscape. I shudder when I hear weather broadcasters refer to some weather as being "nasty" or "bad". I always reported the weather, not judge it. After all, "One man's junk is another man's treasure". Weather is merely the atmosphere's response to the balance, or imbalance, in the forces that have made life possible for humans over thousands of years. Technologies have improved our quality of life, and communication has made it possible for people to prepare and seek shelter from weather extremes.

Journalist Tom Brokaw has said those of us who grew up in the Great Depression, won World War II and rebuilt America, sent man to the moon were part of the greatest generation. Truly we have been blessed in many ways. Now that we are being informed 24/7 with news reports, we see that there is a lot of good, yet so much evil in the world.

While there are some that discount the Bible as being full of a lot of myths, I have found that there is a lot of truth that pertains to human behavior and life in general. There is one side of me related to my religious experiences that I call my "Glory Days". That is what I conclude this memoir with!

Chapter 50 - Glory Days

In reference to my life, I think it relevant that I make mention of my religious beliefs; especially in light of the differences between Judeo/Christian, Muslim, and other faiths during the early 21st century. Like most adults, I attribute my beliefs to my personal search for the meaning of life. Growing up, I learned to be tolerant of other people's views because we all have different life experiences.

It has been said, "Do not pass judgment until you've walked a mile in another man's shoes". I tried to learn about life from the words of Jesus Christ and the lives of successful people like Benjamin Franklin and Thomas Edison. School teachers had a great influence on me. My sixth-grade teacher, Anne Overstreet, taught me "Actions speak louder than words". Our rulers were inscribed with the Golden Rule, "Do unto others, as you would have them do unto you".

I grew up in a time when life's choices were simpler. In public school, our days began with a student reading a passage from the Holy Bible, and we faced the American flag with our hands over our hearts to recite the pledge of allegiance. We were taught to obey the law and respect authority. We attended church where we associated with many godly people. We learned that no one is perfect and that we should be prayerful and confess our sins to God. According to the scriptures, the true church is actually the universal body of believers. On this side of heaven, I have associated with thousands of fellow believers along the way. Here is an account of my journey.

Since childhood, I usually observed the Lord's Day as the time to attend Sunday School and church. In the town of my birth, Pine Beach, NJ, I remember learning my first song "Jesus Loves Me". When visiting my grandmother, Me-Mom Mamie, in Mayetta, NJ, we went to Sunday School in nearby Cedar Run. It was there that I mainly remember the color pictures of Bible stories. My brother Richard and I were taught to memorize a couple of Bible verses, one of which was John 13:34, "A new commandment I give unto you, that you love one another."

In 1941, we first moved to Florida. My brother and I visited the Baptist Church in Green Cove Springs and a summer session called Vacation Bible School. The "hands-on" projects were the main things I remember. When we moved to Jacksonville, I joined my playmate, Jimmy Butts, at the Naval Baptist Church in Yukon, which later was renamed Yukon Baptist Church. Jimmy's father was Sunday School Superintendent.

Our Sunday School teacher was a sailor from the Navy Base, Bob Peterson. At the end of each class, he handed each of us a Bible verse to memorize for the next Sunday. The next time we met, we recited the verse we learned. At the age of 80, I still remember most of those verses, such as Romans 3:23 "All have sinned and come short of the glory of God" and I Corinthians 10:13 "There has no temptation taken you but such as is common to man...but God is faithful and will provide a way that you can endure it".

As a young person, I often visited churches nearby. When my father died in 1946, I stayed at Margaret and Edgar Clancy's house on Park Street where the educational building of Riverside Methodist Church now stands. I attended Dr. Albert Kissling's Riverside Presbyterian Church that stood at the corner of Park and Post Streets. When we moved downtown, I visited First Baptist Church and Snyder Memorial Church near Hemming Park.

Since I didn't drink or smoke, I felt that the Baptist church was for me because the Church Covenant said that (1) we should abstain from drinking alcoholic beverages, and (2) since our bodies are the temple of the Holy Spirit, we should not smoke tobacco because it damages the body (lungs). When I joined the Air Force and was assigned to Chanute Air Force Base, IL, I witnessed a different form of praying. I visited a Nazarene church in Rantoul, IL where the preacher announced, "Let's Pray". To my surprise, the worshipers got up from their seats, walked up and down the aisles with raised their arms with each saying their own prayers. After that, I just attended the Protestant service on the base with my friend Jack Hall.

Upon being assigned to Albany, GA in 1951, I attended the downtown First Baptist Church where I professed my faith on Easter Sunday and was baptized by Dr. Leonard A. Stephens. I was most blessed a year later when I was assigned to Oklahoma A&M College (now Oklahoma State University). I came to know many close friends at the Baptist Student Union.

Under the directions of Rev. Kermit Whitaker, the Vesper Services each evening were very inspiring. We sang hymns and choruses and many students shared their experiences with us. Some of us would gather on Sunday afternoons and visit the city jail and nursing homes to sing gospel songs like "Down by the River Side" and "Mansion over the Hill Top".

Also, I used the piano in the Student Union to teach myself to play a few simple hymns. One of my favorites was "When I Survey the Wondrous Cross". After receiving my assignment to Alaska, I had to meet a 2 AM bus to California. I was very impressed when one of my friends, John Nance, offered to get up at that hour to drive me to the bus station.

1952 Awaiting ship at Camp Stoneman

I spent a month at Camp Stoneman, CA being processed for travel via transport ship to Alaska. During that time, I spent an hour each day learning to play the Hammond Organ in the Base Chapel. It was there that I was assigned to KP (Kitchen Police) where we operated the Cafeteria from 7 AM to 7 PM. We'd mop the floors after each meal, but enjoyed the free food. My favorite was the three-flavored ice cream bars, vanilla, chocolate, and strawberry.

Upon arriving in Anchorage, I was invited to attend a mission that was to become Faith Baptist Church. We gathered in the "hole in the ground" building that was to become the basement of the future church.

Several of us airmen, including Brian Cason, were invited for fellowship at a girl's house whose family had flooded the backyard to create a skating rink. This was something I could never find in Florida! I was at Elmendorf AFB only a month before being sent to Shemya Island near the end of the Aleutian Chain.

There were no worship services there, although there was a chapel with a Hammond organ in one wing of our living quarters. I decided to place a notice on the bulletin board that I would conduct services on Sunday at 11 AM. Around 20 airmen showed up as I started the service playing a few hymns and leading singing. I went up to the pulpit, read a short passage of scripture, and gave a brief talk, hardly a sermon. A few months afterward, a Chaplain visited around once a month to conduct services. I received a Citation for my service to the servicemen there by the Office of the Chaplain in Anchorage.

In 1953, after being discharged from the Air Force and returning to Jacksonville, I visited Riverside Park Baptist Church where Bobby Carter introduced me to his sister, Virginia.

We were attracted to each other so much that some people thought we were brother and sister. We loved children and worked in Sunday School and the Training Union with Junior age kids, mainly 9-year-olds. We were married by Rev. Hubert Taylor there and we and the Taylor family were very close friends for many years later; in fact, Hubert Taylor married our daughter Wendy to Bob Schwank in our living room about 30 years later.

When we moved to Tallahassee and FSU in 1955, we attended First Baptist Church where Dr. Harold Sanders was pastor, and renowned singer Frank Boggs was Music Director. We loved the evening song services where we were often taught a new chorus, such as "I Know A Place" and "I Know the Lord Will Make a Way for Me". When Virginia was expecting our first baby, she came home to live with her parents. I would drive to Jacksonville each weekend and Riverside Park Baptist Church offered to pay me 25 dollars to clean the buildings and play the piano. Congregational singing sounded great in the church because it was a square, wooden building that amplified and blended all the voices.

In 1957, we moved into our new house off Soutel Drive which was closer to my work with the U.S. Weather Bureau at Imeson Airport. We attended Riverview Baptist Church on Lem Turner Road which had a large membership that grew to the point that a second Educational building was built. Virginia sang in the choir which was conducted by well-known pianist Lee Turner. I was Sunday School Superintendent for a year, even though I worked shift work at the airport and sometimes worked the midnight shift. When I became Chief Meteorologist at Channel 4, we started going to North Jacksonville Baptist Church which had a thriving educational program and magnificent music under Leroy Summers.

When we moved in 1965 closer to Channel 4 on Jacksonville's Southside, we found it hard to find a similar Baptist church. Finally, thirteen years later our daughter, Wendy, led us to downtown First Baptist Church. We were part of the real glory days of that congregation. Dr. Homer Lindsay, Sr. had just retired and his son, Homer Lindsay, Jr. led the church to its greatest accomplishments. With over 5,000 in attendance for Sunday School and a new auditorium that could not hold many more than 3,000 members, two morning services were started. The choir, under the leadership of Denney Dawson and his wife, Diane, grew with up to 200 members. We learned new, inspiring choral music for nearly every service. Special musical productions were presented three or four times a year.

The soloists, who were part of our congregation, inspired us each week with meaningful hymns. Wayne Coleman sang "'Til the Storm Passes By", Gloria Robinson sang. Bill Gaither's song "There's Something Different About Him', and Homer Lindsay's sermons touched a chord in the lives of many of us. In fact, occasionally Jimmy Theron's "Amens!" would rise up to the rafters. For five years the choir and church members presented the drama "The Life of Christ". The auditorium was filled Friday and Saturday nights and Sunday.

These experiences were the ultimate in "Glory Days" for many of us during that era. After surviving a heart attack and congestive heart failure, my body was weakened to the point where I had to depend on God to regain enough strength to walk. It began with my counting my blessings as I could barely walk from room to room in my home. I felt the message of the shepherd David applied to me as I was "walking through the valley of the shadow of death" (Psalm 23). The words of the hymns I had learned over the years, such as "He Leadeth Me", and "I Need Thee Every Hour", inspired me as I could

153

finally walk to the sidewalk outside my home. Being able to walk a couple of blocks after two months, I felt the words of "It is no Secret", "Love Lifted Me" and "A Shelter in the Time of Storm" reminded me of God's healing power.

And I must add that through the years, I have been blessed by the friendship, spirituality, and guidance of other men of the cloth. I have known Rev. Dick Petry, Pastor Emeritus First United Methodist Church of Jacksonville since our days at Lake Shore Junior High and Robert E. Lee Senior High. We are members of the Lee High Reunion Committee and together have helped gather former classmates for seven reunions. And as a devoted Methodist minister, he has been unfailing in supporting and enhancing my Southern Baptist Christian faith.

Jacksonville has also been fortunate to have other such outstanding ministers as Albert Kissling of Riverside Presbyterian, Grady Snowden, Jr. of Park Lane Baptist, Richard Petry of Snyder Memorial Methodist Church, and Dr. Homer Lindsay, Sr. and Dr. Homer Lindsay, Jr. of the First Baptist Church. All were compassionate pastors beloved by their congregations and highly respected in the community at large.

I have always considered my religious beliefs to be a personal matter. I believe in the true God of all creation and found that Moses' account of creation was striking familiar with the order of formation of the earth, from the steamy ball that slowly cooled to condense the vapors to the ocean below and the overcast above. By the fourth stage (not a literal day), the clouds separated to reveal the sun, moon, and stars. I found it to be remarkably true the forms of life prior to Homo Sapiens agree with evolutionary science. I disagree with the Fundamentalists that take the Biblical account literally.

I think my religion is closer to that of the Christian Universalists but many who have this conviction continue to attend traditional churches for the sake of remaining united with their families. When it comes down to it, churches have served God's purpose of nurturing morality in the lives of children. After all, Jesus said, "Let the little children come to Him, for of such is the Kingdom of heaven". Jesus was the Great Teacher through his parables. As I grew older, I tried to be tolerant of other people's beliefs. But I've refused to trust the money-seeking appeals of the evangelists who appear on television in my home. They are today's equivalent of the money-changers that Jesus condemned in the synagogues.

154

As I grow older, in some strange way I feel a closeness to friends and family who have passed on before me. While I am still constrained by the bonds of time and distance, my heart can still commune with countless people I've known through life experiences and their influence on my being. There's an old song called "Dear Hearts and Gentle People", published in 1949 with music by Sammy Fain and lyrics by Bob Hilliard.

I love those dear hearts and gentle people
Who live in my hometown
Because those dear hearts and gentle people
Will never ever let you down

They read the good book from Fri' till Monday
That's how the weekend goes
I've got a dream house I'll build there one day
With picket fence and ramblin' rose

I feel so welcome each time that I return
That my happy heart keeps laughin' like a clown
I love the dear hearts and gentle people
Who live and love in my hometown

93472637R00091

Made in the USA
Columbia, SC
10 April 2018